★ ULTIMATE ★

BOOK OF

SPORTS

★ ULTIMATE ★

BOOK OF

SPORTS

The Essential Collection

OF RULES, STATS, AND TRIVIA
FOR OVER 250 SPORTS

BY SCOTT McNEELY

ILLUSTRATIONS BY ARTHUR MOUNT

CHRONICLE BOOKS

SAN FRANCISCO

Text copyright © 2012 by Scott McNeely
Illustrations copyright © 2012 by Arthur Mount

Library of Congress Cataloging-in-Publication Data

McNeely, Scott.
  The ultimate book of sports / Scott McNeely.
      p. cm.
  ISBN 978-1-4521-1059-2
  1. Sports—Miscellanea. 2. Sports—Rules. I. Title.
  GV707.M398 2012
  796—dc23

                                        2011053161

Manufactured in China

Designed by Warmbo Design

10 9 8 7 6 5 4 3 2

Chronicle Books
680 Second Street
San Francisco, CA 94107

www.chroniclebooks.com

DEDICATION

For Emmett and Hollis

*I'm not saying I want my two boys playing professional football
or baseball. Yet as a dad, the most important gift I can
give my kids is just enough information to be dangerous
playing most any sport that exists.*

CONTENTS

FOREWORD P.12

WHAT IS A SPORT? P.15

AUTO RACING P.29
DRAG RACING P.30
FORMULA RACING P.31
MONSTER TRUCK P.32
RALLY RACING P.33
SPORTS CAR RACING P.34
STOCK CAR RACING P.35

BALL, NET, AND DISC P.39
AUSTRALIAN RULES FOOTBALL P.40
BASKETBALL P.43
» Korfball p.50
DODGEBALL P.51
FOUR SQUARE P.54
HANDBALL P.56
» American Handball p.58

KICKBALL P.59
NETBALL P.62
» Indoor Netball p.65
TETHERBALL P.65
» Swingball p.67
ULTIMATE P.67
» Disc Golf p.69
VOLLEYBALL P.70
» Beach Volleyball p.74

BASEBALL P.77
MAJOR LEAGUE BASEBALL P.78
ROUNDERS P.87

BOATING AND ROWING P.89
DRAGON BOAT RACING P.90
ROWING P.92
» Sculling p.95
YACHT RACING P.96

BOWLING AND CURLING P.101

PÉTANQUE P.102
- » Bocce p.104
- » Lawn Bowling p.105

CURLING P.106

SHUFFLEBOARD P.108

TEN-PIN BOWLING P.110
- » Nine-Pin Bowling p.112
- » Five-Pin Bowling p.113
- » Candlepin Bowling p.113

COMBAT SPORTS P.115

MARTIAL ARTS P.116
- » Aikido p.117
- » Capoeira p.117
- » Judo p.118
- » Jujitsu p.118
- » Karate p.120
- » Kendo p.121
- » Nguni Stick Fighting p.121
- » Tae Kwon Do p.122

BOXING P.123
- » Kickboxing p.127
- » Muay Thai p.127

FENCING P.130

CUE SPORTS P.133

CUSHION BILLIARDS P.134

POOL P.136
- » Straight Pool p.140
- » Nine-Ball p.141
- » Bumper Pool p.141

SNOOKER P.142

CYCLING P.147

BMX P.148

MOUNTAIN BIKING P.150

ROAD RACING P.151

TRACK CYCLING P.153

EQUESTRIAN SPORTS P.157

HORSE RACING P.158
- » Thoroughbred Racing p.160
- » Quarter Horse Racing p.160
- » Steeplechase p.160
- » Harness Racing p.161

OLYMPIC COMPETITIONS P.161
» Dressage p.161
» Eventing p.162
» Show Jumping p.162

POLO P.163
» Arena Polo p.164

RODEO RIDING P.165
» Barrel Racing p.165
» Bronc and Bull Riding p.165
» Roping p.167
» Steer Wrestling p.167

VAULTING P.168

FICTIONAL SPORTS P.171

TERRESTRIAL SPORTS P.172
» BASEketball p.173
» Death Race p.173
» Futuresport p.173
» Gumball Rally p.174
» Jugger p.174
» Rollerball p.174
» Running Man p.175

INTERSTELLAR AND MYTHICAL
SPORTS P.175
» Brockian Ultra-Cricket p.176
» Flamingo Croquet p.176
» German Batball p.176
» Podracing p.176
» Quidditch p.177
» Triad p.177
» Tron p.178
» Tsunkatse p.178

FOOTBALL AND RUGBY P.181

AMERICAN FOOTBALL P.182
» Canadian Football p.188

RUGBY UNION P.189
» Rugby Sevens p.195

RUGBY LEAGUE P.195

GOLF P.199

STROKE PLAY P.200
» Match Play p.207
» Skins p.207

GYMNASTICS P.209

ARTISTIC P.210
» Balance Beam p.211
» Floor Exercise p.211
» Horizontal Bar p.212
» Parallel Bars p.212
» Pommel Horse p.212
» Rings p.213
» Uneven Bars p.213
» Vault p.213

RHYTHMIC P.215
TRAMPOLINE P.216

HOCKEY P.219

FIELD HOCKEY P.220
» Indoor Field Hockey p.222

ICE HOCKEY P.223
» Street Hockey p.228

MOTORCYCLE RACING P.231

ROAD RACING P.232
  » Grands Prix p.233
  » Superbike p.233
  » Supersport p.233
  » Superstock p.234
  » Sidecar p.234
  » Endurance p.234

MOTOCROSS P.235
  » Freestyle p.235
  » MX1/MX2/M3 p.236
  » Sidecarcross p.236
  » Supercross p.236
  » Supermoto p.236

ENDURO P.237
TRACK RACING P.238
  » Speedway p.238
  » Flat Track p.238
  » Quarter Mile p.239

MULTI-DISCIPLINE SPORTS P.241

BIATHLON P.242
TRIATHLON P.244
PENTATHLON P.245
HEPTATHLON P.246
DECATHLON P.247

ODDBALL SPORTS P.249

AIR GUITAR P.250
ARM WRESTLING P.251
BATON TWIRLING P.252
BOG SNORKELING P.254
BOOMERANG THROWING P.255
CAMEL RACING P.256
CHEERLEADING P.257
CHESSBOXING P.258
COMPETITIVE EATING P.259
DEMOLITION DERBY P.261
DRUMLINES P.262
EXTREME IRONING P.263
LUMBERJACKING P.264
MAN VS. HORSE MARATHON P.265
SOAPBOX RACING P.266
TRACTOR PULLING P.267
WIFE CARRYING P.268
ZORBING P.269

RACQUET, PADDLE, AND STICK P.271

BADMINTON P.272
CRICKET P.275
  » Limited Overs p.280

CROQUET P.280
  » Association Croquet p.280
  » Golf Croquet p.281

HURLING P.282
LACROSSE P.284
  » Field Lacrosse p.284
  » Box Lacrosse p.286

PELOTA P.286
» Hand Pelota p.286
» Paleta Goma p.287
» Jai Alai p.287

RACQUETBALL P.288
» Paddleball p.290

SQUASH P.290
TABLE TENNIS P.292
TENNIS P.294

RUNNING, JUMPING, AND THROWING P.301

CROSS COUNTRY P.302
ROAD RUNNING P.303
TRACK AND FIELD P.304
» Sprints p.305
» Middle Distance p.305
» Long Distance p.305
» Hurdles p.305
» Steeplechase p.306
» Relay p.306
» Long Jump p.306
» Triple Jump p.307
» High Jump p.307
» Pole Vaulting p.307
» Discus Throw p.307
» Shot Put p.308
» Javelin Throw p.308
» Hammer Throw p.308
RACE WALKING P.309

SKATING P.311

ICE SKATING P.312
» Figure Skating p.313
» Speed Skating p.313

IN-LINE SKATING P.314
» In-line Speed Skating p.314
» In-line Downhill Skating p.315
» In-line Freestyle Skating p.315

ROLLER SKATING P.315
» Artistic Skating p.316
» Rink Hockey p.316
» Roller Derby p.316

SKATEBOARDING P.317

SKI AND SNOW P.321

ALPINE SKIING P.322
» Slalom p.323
» Giant Slalom p.323
» Super-Giant Slalom p.323
» Downhill p.323
» Freestyle p.323
» Ski Jumping p.324

CROSS-COUNTRY SKIING P.324
COMPETITIVE SLEDDING P.325
» Bobsled p.325
» Luge p.326
» Skeleton p.326

DOGSLED RACING P.326
SNOWBOARDING P.327

SOCCER P.329

ASSOCIATION FOOTBALL P.330
GAELIC FOOTBALL P.338

TARGET SPORTS P.341

ARCHERY P.342
DARTS P.343
SHOOTING P.345

WATER SPORTS P.347

COMPETITIVE SWIMMING P.348
» Backstroke p.348
» Breaststroke p.349
» Butterfly p.349
» Freestyle p.350

SYNCHRONIZED SWIMMING P.351
PLATFORM DIVING P.352
» Springboard Diving p.353
» Synchronized Diving p.354

SURFING P.354
WATERSKIING P.355
WATER POLO P.356

WRESTLING AND WEIGHTLIFTING P.359

FREESTYLE WRESTLING P.360
GRECO-ROMAN WRESTLING P.361
OIL WRESTLING P.362
SUMO P.363
WEIGHTLIFTING P.365
» Snatch p.365
» Clean and Jerk p.365

YE OLDE SPORTS P.367

CHARIOT RACING P.368
GLADIATOR COMBAT P.369
JOUSTING P.370
NAUMACHIA P.371
PANKRATION P.372
PITZ P.373
SKITTLES P.373
TUG OF HOOP P.374
TUG OF WAR P.375

ABOUT THE AUTHOR P.376

Foreword

I'VE NEVER BEEN PARTICULARLY GOOD AT SPORTS.

In the second grade I did invent a game called Trip Potty. I was the "potty" and classmates would chase me mercilessly at recess in order to trip me. It was easy pickings, owing to the fact that I wore a kind of Dickensian corrective shoe for reasons that elude me to this very day.

In my family it was my grandfather who was Mr. Sporty. He excelled in *every* sport and even bagged a handful of world record fish. He must have wondered what happened to his sports gene, why it expressed itself so feebly in me.

Perhaps I redeemed myself by playing ice hockey as a preteen and by joining my high school's wrestling and fencing teams (*en garde!*). Yet I never had the passion of a true sportsman. I rarely watched sports on television. I never wore a football jersey to school.

So why did I write an entire book about sports?

Oddly enough I love the drama of sports. I remember watching my first professional soccer game, at Stamford Bridge in London, the rabid Chelsea fans unlike any I had ever encountered. I remember my first Oakland Raiders football game from the infamous "black hole" section of the stadium, my first Aussie rules footy game at the MCG surrounded by maniacal Essendon fans, my first World Cup soccer match watching from a pub in Ireland as the Irish defeated Romania 5–4 on penalty kicks. Over and over again I've learned that sports are chock-full of passion-fueled moments. And I've learned that passionate people can easily connect with sports.

In my travels I've been lucky enough to encounter many less-heralded sports, too: oil wrestling in Turkey, camel racing in India, kickboxing in Thailand. For me that's the magic formula, getting caught up in a swirl of emotion and using sport as a lens to access the broader culture (yours or somebody else's). With this perspective in mind, sports are never dull and can never disappoint.

—*SCOTT MCNEELY*

>>

What Is a Sport?

>>

DICTIONARY.COM DEFINES "SPORT" as "an athletic activity requiring skill or physical prowess and often of a competitive nature, such as racing, baseball, tennis, golf, bowling, wrestling, boxing, hunting, fishing, etc."

Kinda sorta. We beg to differ on the finer points.

Certainly we agree that sports are, by definition, physical activities. This is why chess, poker, and similar games are not included in this book. We also agree that sports must be competitive in nature. Sports must produce winners and losers.

Where we differ is in the last two examples listed. Hunting and fishing? Not so much. We classify these as mere activities. The reason? To qualify as a sport, an activity must pit one or more people in *direct* competition. And the word "direct" is critical here. Of course it is possible to transform any activity into a competition. Yet true sports involve humans competing directly with other humans.

Sure, hunters compete to bag the largest game. But let's be honest, the essence of hunting is the competition between *hunter* and *prey*. The fact that my deer/bear/duck/fox has larger horns/weighs more/is quackier/has a fluffier tail is not the point.

It's a similar situation with fishing. True, there are official tournaments and competitions. And true, fishermen compete to catch the largest fish. Yet labeling fishing a sport is a like making a sport of panning for gold. If my gold nugget or fish is larger than yours, it's generally blind luck or technology that's responsible. My ability to exert an influence over the outcome is minimal. You might as well make a sport out of trainspotting or sunset watching.

WHY ISN'T WWF WRESTLING IN THIS BOOK?

SO ACCORDING TO THE DEFINITION ABOVE, sports like the World Wrestling Federation should get a mention in this book, right?

Nope. The final requirement of a true sport is real—as opposed to staged—conflict. Certainly sports entertain, but they are not entertainments. WWF wrestling is more heavily scripted than a daytime soap opera and there's no actual competition involved—plenty of physical skill, but no authentic conflict or competition.

It's no different with reality television shows such as *The Amazing Race, Dancing with the Stars, Survivor, Fear Factor,* and a million lookalike programs. Though they often wear the trappings of sports-like pursuits, reality-television sports are artificial by their nature. You can't participate unless you're a specially selected contestant. And the competition ends as soon as the television show is canceled

ANY ACTIVITY CAN BE TURNED into a competition. So what makes a sport a sport? In this book a sport is any physical activity, governed by rules, involving authentic and direct competition between one or more people.

by the network. Except in reruns on late-night cable, there is no sporting future for *American Gladiator* and its ilk.

There are two final sports-like categories officially excluded from this book: competitive games and cultural art forms. The former includes hide-and-seek, geocaching, laser tag, miniature golf, go-cart racing, and countless other "sporting activities" that operate purely in the realm of fun. There's no such thing as a professional go-cart racer or a laser tag athlete. If either title does apply to you, immediately contact your local therapist for some much-needed hugging.

Cultural art forms include activities such as bullfighting and snake charming, as well as religious and cultural festivals such as the running of the bulls in Pamplona (Spain), tomato throwing festival in Buñol (Spain), palm tree climbing competition in Jakarta (Indonesia), World Egg Throwing Championships in Swaton (England), World Sauna Championships in Heinola (Finland), and the World's Ugliest Dog Contest in California. These events are all plenty of fun. But none qualify as a true sport.

A BRIEF HISTORY OF SPORTS

SPORTS ARE AS OLD AS MANKIND. Archaeological evidence from cave paintings made twenty thousand years ago suggests that games of throwing, catching, jumping, and stick-fighting have evolved alongside humans. Sports, it seems, are simply part of what makes us human, like opposable thumbs and highly developed brains.

True competitive sports show up in nearly every ancient civilization. Wall paintings in an 1850 BC Egyptian tomb include images of wrestlers demonstrating holds still used today, as well as ball games that look mighty similar to modern handball. The ancient Egyptians— at least the upper classes with enough leisure time to spare—were also keen javelin throwers, archers, rowers, swimmers, and long-distance runners. The ancient Egyptians knew how to stay fit.

The ancient Greeks had a healthy admiration for the human form and literally worshipped their athletes. The fullest expression of this near-fanatical worship of sport is the world's very first athletic competition: the games held in 776 BC at Olympia (home to the sanctuary of Zeus, the Greeks' mightiest god). The games were held every four years, and soon the original Olympic footrace was augmented with discus and javelin throwing, boxing, wrestling, and chariot and horse racing. The athletes competed for glory, as the traditional prize was just a wreath woven from olive branches. The ancient Olympics lasted for more than a thousand years until AD 393—a remarkable run for any sporting event.

In the Roman era sports were a primary source of entertainment for the empire's potentially unruly citizens. Gladiator fights and mock land-and-sea battles were not about promoting athleticism. Instead they provided the ancient equivalent of an opiate for the working classes.

It was a very different situation in ancient China and Japan, where sports were more commonly used to train future warriors in the arts of sword fighting, horse riding, and hand-to-hand combat. Probably the world's oldest organized team sport is polo, which originated in Persia in the second century BC to train horsemen for the Persian cavalry.

It's not until the fourteenth century that people had enough leisure time to devote to games and sports on feast days and during village celebrations. The many related games of "bowls" date from this era, all involving rolling round objects close to—but not touching—a target.

Tennis is the next big innovation in sports. Monks in sixteenth-century France stretched a rope across the monastery courtyard and used their hands to hit a ball. Gloves were used later and eventually players started to use short bats. England's King Henry VII became

ARCHERY, THE ORIGINAL 2ND AMENDMENT

ORGANIZED SPORTS IN EUROPE disappeared after the fall of the Roman Empire. Even throughout the Middle Ages people had little time for sports—they were too busy dying of the plague or dying in the Crusades or dying in childbirth. The one exception was archery, which was highly encouraged even among the poor as a form of militia training.

a passionate player and built many "royal courts" to slake his tennis thirst. Following tennis, new sports such as curling, billiards, golf, and horse racing became fashionable.

In the nineteenth century, average working-class people got their first chance to participate in organized sports. As the industrial revolution swept through Europe and the United States, rules limiting work to half-days on Saturdays, for example, became commonplace. As organized sports became more accessible, the narrative of sports changed, too. It was accepted that sports developed character and morality; that sporting competitions should be fair and governed by rules; that sports are rewards unto themselves and should not be played for money. This was the golden era of amateurism in sport, perfectly embodied by the reestablishment of the modern Olympics in 1896.

In the twentieth century many sports enjoyed phenomenal growth thanks to booming post–World War II economies and the spread of television. Baseball, basketball, American football, soccer, auto racing—pretty much every major sport in the American pantheon experienced rapid growth throughout the 1950s and '60s as television ownership soared. Every major television network competed aggressively for broadcast rights (and the accompanying advertising space) to major games and championships. With this newfound popularity came money, lots of it.

The concept of "amateurism" in sports, of athletes who receive no compensation but perform for the love of their sport, was dying a slow death throughout the late twentieth century. The Olympics had nominally been an amateur-only competition for the first half of the twentieth century (athlete Jim Thorpe scandalously had his 1912 medals revoked for accepting compensation as a minor league baseball player). However, in the 1970s the International Olympic Committee (IOC) acknowledged the growing reality of money in

TOP 5 BIGGEST
SPORTING SCANDALS, EVER

★ **"BLACK SOX SCANDAL"
 AT THE 1919 WORLD SERIES.**
 It was the Chicago White Sox versus the Cincinnati
 Reds. At the time baseball was America's most
 popular sport—nothing else even came close.
 Eight players on the White Sox (including Shoeless
 Joe Jackson, whose involvement has since been
 disputed) were accused of purposely losing games
 and were suspended from baseball for life. The
 scandal stunned the country. No sports scandal
 has ever had such a profound effect on the national
 psyche.

★ **THE HAND OF GOD.**
 It was a 1986 quarterfinal World Cup soccer match
 between Argentina and England. The score was
 0-0 in the fifty-first minute when Argentina's most
 famous player, Diego Maradona, received a pass
 in front of England's goal and—oops!—tapped

the ball in with his hand. The referee missed the flagrant violation; millions of people watching on television did not. Amid boos and protests on the field, Argentina won the match thanks in part to a second, near-perfect, and totally legal goal from Maradona. Argentina went on to win the World Cup trophy. Maradona later admitted to cheating but claimed it was the "hand of God" that knocked the ball into the net.

★ **TONYA HARDING WHACKS NANCY KERRIGAN.**
One month before the 1994 Winter Olympics, figure skater Nancy Kerrigan was bashed in the knee at the end of a skating practice. The attacker? A man hired by the then-husband of figure skater—and Olympic competitor—Tonya Harding. It's debatable whether Harding knew of the attack beforehand. But it's certain she lied to police afterwards. Kerrigan finished second. Harding wept on the ice and placed eighth and was later banned for life from skating. The story became a tabloid sensation.

★ **CHEATING AT THE PARALYMPICS.**
Yes, it happened at the 2000 Paralympic Games when the Spanish basketball team won gold in the "intellectual disability" category. The problem?

Ten of the team's twelve players had no disability. "We were encouraged to pretend to be stupid," player Carlos Ribagorda said after the hoax was uncovered and the team was forced to return its gold medals.

★ **RACISM AND DRUGS.**
We're bucketing up all the ugliness of professional sports into a single category. On the racism front, the medal of shame is awarded jointly to cricket (for the shocking treatment of black cricketer Basil D'Oliveira during the South African apartheid era) and to the International Olympic Committee for stripping Jim Thorpe (the first Native American Olympic medalist) of his 1912 Olympic medals on a flimsy charge of violating the amateur athlete rules. There are far too many drugs scandals to list, but let's just agree that Barry Bonds, Mark McGwire, the disgraced 2007 Tour de France teams, Lance Armstrong, Konstantinos Kenteris, Ekaterini Thanou, Diego Maradona, and all the other players who take performance-enhancing drugs in blatant disregard of the rules and esprit of sport—let's agree that they all suck.

all levels of sports and relaxed its rules barring professional athletes. By 1988 every international Olympics sporting federation, minus wrestling and boxing, allowed its professional athletes to compete.

Another symptom of the influx of television money into sport was the obscenely paid sports superstar. One example: the average annual salary of an NFL player was $6,000 in the 1950s, $10,000 in the 1970s, $198,000 in the 1980s, $785,000 in the 1990s, and more than $2 million today. These are *average* salaries; at the high end the numbers get astronomical (NFL player Michael Vick was awarded a ten-year, $130 million contract in 2005, which doesn't even come close to the $275 million Alex Rodriguez is guaranteed for playing Major League Baseball for ten years).

Spectators have a love-hate relationship with superstars. On one hand they love to watch them perform. Michael Jordan, Lance Armstrong, David Beckham, Tiger Woods, Shane Warne—who doesn't love to watch superstar athletes perform at their peak. On the other hand, superstars seem divorced from reality, distant, untouchable—a far cry from the amateur class of athletes who dominated sports for so many years.

It's hard to predict the future direction of sports. Are we doomed to a future with *Rollerball*-like mega-corporations concocting mindless sporting competitions to keep the masses in check? Or is the future of sport more noble, more hopeful? It's hard to know. All we can say for certain is that sports fans will continue to watch the spectacles unfold on whatever devices are handy.

IF I'M A SPORTS HATER,
SHOULD I STOP READING NOW?

OKAY, GOT IT. YOU HATE SPORTS. Now just for fun, list a few reasons why sports make your blood boil.

> » *I get yelled at when I want to watch the Emmys instead of football.*
>
> » *Game seven is* always *more important than [fill in the blank].*
>
> » *When someone at the office asks, "Did you see the game last night?" or says, "I can't believe they made that trade," or shouts, "Go Yankees!" I want to puke.*
>
> » *Cheerleaders' uniforms (buxom breasts do not win games).*
>
> » *I want people to stop screaming and yelling at my television.*
>
> » *Sports are boring until someone starts a fight or gets injured.*
>
> » *Professional athletes are so incredibly full of themselves.*
>
> » *The movies* The Rookie, Invincible, Miracle, A League of Their Own, Tin Cup, *and* Bull Durham *should never have been made.*
>
> » *Sports fill me with ennui, boredom, and bored ennui.*

Fair enough, these are valid reasons not to love sports.

Yet before you toss aside this book and close its cover forever, let me say one thing. Don't get caught up in the male-dominated machismo surrounding most sports. Don't get lost in the players' supersized egos or the dimestore philosophizing of the twenty-four-hour sports media. None of that stuff matters.

Instead, focus on the *promise* of sports (even when it goes unfulfilled). Sports, at their very best, promise to:

» **Instill good sportsmanship:** *Where else are you going to learn how to own up to your mistakes and apologize? Athletes do it all the time.*

» **Leave lasting impressions:** *Sports provide real-life drama, a captured moment of something incredible indelibly etched on your memory. This is 100 percent guaranteed: if your kids catch a fly ball at a baseball game, they will remember it for the rest of their lives.*

» **Connect people:** *Sports can bond two complete strangers over little more than a common appreciation of a sport, a player, a home team. Sports create friendships and camaraderie. The beer helps, too.*

» **Make men cry:** *Sports bring out emotions that most men would otherwise never experience. Your team loses? Cry. Your team wins? Cry.*

» **Provide endless entertainment:** *Love the magnitude. Love the spectacle. Love the halftime performance.*

» **Let us be kids again:** *For better or worse, the fastest way to channel your third-grade self is to grab a bat, basketball, football, handball, or other sporting implement, and simply have a go. Metaphorically you're doomed to either strike out or hit a home run. Either way, you've forgotten about the hardships and heartbreaks of life—and instantly you're a kid again.*

Approach the rest of this book in a similar spirit and you will not be disappointed by sports.

01

Auto Racing

CHAPTER ONE

DRAG RACING

----- DON'T BLINK, YOU'LL MISS IT -----

ASK YOUR PARENTS ABOUT THE 1950S. Apparently back then kids ate hamburgers at drive-ins, kissed in the backseats of borrowed convertibles, and spent Saturday nights watching cars race illegally on city streets. By 1953 the National Hot Rod Association (NHRA; www.nhra.com) was formed to discourage street racing in favor of competitive drag racing. The NHRA also oversaw some of the sport's loosely organized competitions, including the famed anarchic races at Bonneville Salt Flats.

The basic idea in drag racing is for two cars to race in a straight line from a standing start—it's a test of acceleration more than of speed. Vehicles range from standard street cars to custom-built racing dragsters, depending on the category being contested. Distances range from the traditional quarter-mile track to the eighth-mile track. The fastest times for the quarter-mile run are less than five seconds, which means racers can easily hit a top speed of 320 miles per hour.

FORMULA RACING

----- LISTEN FOR THE F1 RACER: WEEEEEEEEEEEEEEEEEE -----

THE KEY THING TO KNOW ABOUT EVERY FORMULA RACE—from the famous Formula One series down to an amateur club rally—is that formula cars are single-seaters and have open wheelbases. That's simply what it means to be a "formula" racer. Modern cars also feature airfoils in front to produce downlift, which helps cars maintain traction through turns.

The sport's premier event, and the most competitive category, is Formula One (F1). It's governed by the Fédération Internationale de l'Automobile (FIA; www.fia.com) and consists of a series of Grand Prix races held worldwide on purpose-built circuits in cities such as Monaco, Monza, Melbourne, Valencia, and Singapore. F1 is considered the fastest circuit-racing discipline with cars easily achieving speeds of up to 220 miles per hour. F1 is also a global marketing phenomenon: the annual FIA Formula One World Championship reaches television audiences that rival the FIFA World Cup in soccer.

MONSTER TRUCK

----- SUNDAY! SUNDAY! SUNDAY! -----

AH, THE GLORIOUS 1970S! Back in the early 1970s pickup trucks were all the rage. To celebrate the wondrousness that is a pickup truck, some owners started tricking out their rides with 4- and 5-foot-diameter tires. Woo hoo!

Naturally, with tires that large, you also need to CRUSH stuff. Enter trucks with names like Big Foot and King Kong, doing donuts, wheelstands, and big-air jumps in front of massive crowds, absolutely and literally CRUSHING puny street cars underneath their gargantuan TIRES of DEATH (you're doomed, little Honda Accord, mwah ha ha ha).

The radical entertainment value of monster truck racing may have faded in the last three decades, but don't underestimate the public's appetite for watching modified trucks with extremely large wheels and whacked-out suspensions. Monster truck competitions very much are alive and well.

RALLY RACING

THE TYPICAL RALLY RACE is held on an off-road and rough-terrain course. The goal is to complete the predetermined race stages (typically races have fifteen to twenty stages and last two to four days) in the lowest elapsed time. Race vehicles range from so-called Group N cars (basically something you could drive off a showroom floor, completely street-legal and essentially unmodified) to Group A cars (street-legal but with significant performance modifications allowed) according to how the FIA classifies cars.

Rally drivers and codrivers work as a team, one managing the vehicle while the other manages the course and its innumerable obstacles. The FIA-sanctioned World Rally Championship (WRC; www.wrc.com) is the sport's top competitive series, comprising a dozen or so annual rallies held in locations across the globe. Other longstanding rally races include the Dakar Rally (now run in South America due to political instability on its former, traditional Paris-to-Dakar route) and the British Rally Championship.

SPORTS CAR RACING

THE WORLD OF SPORTS CAR RACING is split in two, between the grand tourers (GTs) and the sports prototypes. The former are street-legal cars based on production/showroom models (with performance tweaks, of course). The latter are definitely *not* street-legal cars (most prototypes are just that—flights of fancy from publicity-seeking manufacturers such as Ferrari, Maserati, Mercedes-Benz, and Porsche). Both types of races are run on closed circuits.

The FIA (the sport's governing body) has battled but failed over the past decade to reinstate sports car racing's premier competitive series, the defunct World Sportscar Championship. Historically, teams of racers would compete in 12- to 24-hour qualifying events such as the 24 Hours of Le Mans, Rolex 24 at Daytona, and the 12 Hours of Sebring, with the team earning the most points crowned World Sportscar Champion. These popular racing events still exist, but a World Sportscar Champion has not been crowned since the 1990s due to management missteps at the FIA (sorry, but the truth hurts). The FIA is trying to reinvigorate sports car racing with the new FIA World Endurance Championship, which kicks off its inaugural season in 2012.

STOCK CAR RACING

----- GOD BLESS AMERICA AND NASCAR -----

STOCK RACING IS THE MOST POPULAR FORM OF AUTO RACING in the United States, thanks in no small part to the marketing savvy of the National Association for Stock Car Auto Racing (NASCAR; www.nascar.com). NASCAR sanctions the sport's premier events—including the Daytona 500, Coca-Cola 600, and the Brickyard 400, part of the 36-race annual series that make up the NASCAR Sprint Cup— and through aggressive television distribution has elevated stock car racing to the second-most watched sport in America (behind football). A visit to a NASCAR event is de rigueur for politicians looking for middle America's stamp of approval.

Originally a "stock car" meant any vehicle in its original showroom, factory configuration—in the early days of stock car racing you could literally drive up in your personal car and join a race! Those days are long gone, and nowadays all stock cars are essentially modified

★ NASCAR's first official race was at the North Carolina fairgrounds in Charlotte, in 1949. The winner, Jim Roper, won the race driving a Lincoln Cosmopolitan.

★ NASCAR's first televised race was the 1960 Daytona 500.

★ Richard Petty, the king of NASCAR with two hundred career racing wins, is credited with inventing the window net to help keep drivers' arms inside the car to avoid injuries during a crash.

★ Richard Petty and Dale Earnhardt both won NASCAR championships a record seven times.

★ Temperatures inside a stock car can reach 140° Fahrenheit during a race. And drivers typically lose five to ten pounds in body weight over the course of a race.

★ A NASCAR pit crew usually consists of six members: two tire changers, two tire carriers, a jackman, and a fueler. Pit crews used to have seven members, but the wonderfully named "gas catch-can man" was made obsolete in 2010 (a newly designed gas can no longer requires the catcher).

versions of standard production vehicles. Today's "street stock" class is as close to standard production vehicles as it gets (all cars at a minimum must have unmodified hoods, roofs, and trunks, plus cages and roll bars for safety). Super stock and "late model" classes allow more modifications, though always to strict specifications.

Most stock tracks are oval, and the major races run multiple laps to create race distances of 200 to 600 miles. The average top speeds in premier NASCAR stock events are 190 to 200 miles per hour. The top official speed recorded by NASCAR is a neck-whipping 228 miles per hour.

02

★ ······· 02 ······· ★

≫≫≫

Ball, Net, and Disc

CHAPTER TWO

≫≫≫

AUSTRALIAN RULES FOOTBALL

AUSSIE RULES FOOTBALL, or footy as the sport is informally known, is a pure and beautiful Australian invention. While it borrows aspects from many sports (notably rugby and Gaelic football), footy is remarkably unique in the world of professional sports.

Goalkeepers? No way, who needs 'em! Players with fixed positions? So boring—players are instead free to roam the entire field.

Players can even pick up and kick the ball *or* run with the ball as long as the ball touches ground or is bounced (basketball-style) once every 15 meters. Players can also pass the ball in any direction with an open-hand tap or by punching it with a closed fist (all types of overarm passing are illegal).

Not only that, but footy is physical. Extremely physical. Scrums of players jump into the air standing on each other's shoulders, tackle from behind, you name it. Footy players wear neither helmets nor protective padding. Go Aussie!

The largest professional league is the Australian Football League (AFL; www.afl.com.au), which hosts the annual AFL Grand Final, footy's most prestigious competition where the premiership (league championship) is decided. Befitting Melbourne's status as the city where Aussie rules was first played, the city is home to nine of the AFL's eighteen teams.

★ **BASIC CONCEPT:**

Two teams of eighteen players compete to score points by kicking or punching a ball through goalposts. There are no fixed positions, no offside, and players can use any part of their body to legally move the ball forward or backward on the field. One of the only things players can-not do is throw the ball with an overarm motion; only open-hand taps and closed-fist punches are allowed.

Footy is a fast-moving game, with frequent changes of possession that do not stop the game clock (similar to soccer, only goals, major injuries, out-of-play balls, and when the umpire is setting the angle of a free kick on goal stop the game clock). AFL games are divided into 20-minute quarters.

★ **EQUIPMENT AND PLAYING SPACE:**

Footy is typically played on converted cricket grounds. The Melbourne Cricket Ground (MCG), for example, is the most famous playing field in AFL football. The ball resembles a rugby ball, with an oblong shape and rounded corners that make it easier to bounce and pass. Despite the sport's physical nature, no special equipment or protective gear is worn.

Players can run with the ball as long as they touch the ball to the ground, or bounce it to themselves, once every 15 meters. Players can "mark" the ball (catch it from a kick), which earns the receiver either a free, unobstructed kick from where the ball is caught or the option to "play on" and continue moving with the ball.

Footy is a highly physical sport, with frequent bumps and tackles. When tackled, a player in possession of the ball must dispose of the ball quickly (either by passing or simply letting go). Otherwise the player will earn a foul for holding the ball.

Footy goals are divided into three sections: a central goal and two side goals. Goals, worth 6 points, are scored when the ball is kicked through the central goalposts of the opposing team's goal. It's okay if the ball bounces first. However, only 1 point is earned if the ball is touched (after the kick) by any player or if the ball was kicked by the defending team.

The side goalposts (known as "behind" posts) always score just 1 point. Footy scores list both goals and behinds, so a team with a score of 6.12 (48) has 6 goals (worth 36 points) and 12 behinds (worth 12 points) for a total of 48 points. The team with the higher total score at the end of the match wins.

BASKETBALL

----- "EVEN WHEN I'M OLD AND GRAY, I WON'T BE ABLE TO -----
PLAY IT, BUT I'LL STILL LOVE THE GAME."
—MICHAEL JORDAN

THE BIRTH OF BASKETBALL IS LEGENDARY. On a rainy day in 1891, James Naismith was looking for a way to entertain a group of boys inside a gym at the international Young Men's Christian Association (YMCA) training school in Massachusetts. He hammered a peach basket to the wall about ten feet off the ground and—voilà! Basketball was born. The original balls were soccer balls, not famous for their bouncing qualities. So passing and running—not dribbling—dominated the early game. In fact, dribbling didn't become important until the early 1950s when the modern (and fully round—duh!) basketball was introduced.

The sport quickly took off, especially in rain-soaked New England. By the late 1930s basketball was played at dozens of American colleges and universities (the first NCAA tournament was held in 1939). The National Basketball Association (NBA; www.nba.com) was formed in 1949 to give amateur teams such as the Harlem Globetrotters (from Chicago) and the New York Knickerbockers (predecessor of today's New York Knicks) a professional platform including steady salaries and consistent rules.

Basketball is an American invention, yet the sport has always had a strong international following. The International Basketball Association (FIBA; www.fiba.com), the sport's international governing body, was formed in 1932 with eight founding members: Switzerland, the former Czechoslovakia, Greece, Italy, Latvia, Portugal, Romania, and Argentina. Men's basketball was included as a demonstration sport at the 1904 Olympics and has been a full-medal sport since the 1936 Berlin Olympics. Interestingly, FIBA dropped the distinction between amateurs and professionals in 1986 (highly controversial in some quarters), which has allowed professional NBA players to compete at the Olympics since 1992.

Somewhat predictably, the United States dominated the early pro-inclusive Olympics competitions (the all-NBA "Dream Team" swept and won the gold medal at the '92 Olympics). Yet one sign of the sport's deep international roots is that the United States is no longer invincible: an all-NBA team finished sixth at the 2002 World FIBA Championship and the U.S. men's team took a mere bronze (not the expected gold) at the 2004 Olympics. The men came back to win gold at both the 2008 Olympics and 2010 FIBA World Championship.

Women have played basketball from the sport's earliest days; the first intercollegiate women's basketball game between Stanford and U.C. Berkeley was played in 1896 (Stanford won). Women's basketball was added to the Olympics in 1976.

★ **BASIC CONCEPT**:

Two teams of five try to score points by shooting or "dunking" a basketball into the opponent's hoop, which is set 10 feet above the ground. Players score a "field goal" that's worth either 2 or 3 points, depending on how close they are to the hoop when shooting the ball. Teams move the ball by dribbling or bouncing the ball as they walk or run, and by passing the ball in any direction to a teammate.

NBA games are played in 12-minute quarters. The clock is not continuous and stops whenever there's a time-out or any break in action.

★ ★ ★ ★ ★ ·········· U.B.S. ·········· ★ ★ ★ ★ ★

BASKETBALL

Player substitutions are unlimited but can only be done when the game clock is stopped. Ties are not allowed and are settled in as many 5-minute overtime periods as needed to produce a winner.

★ **EQUIPMENT AND PLAYING SPACE:**

An official NBA basketball court is 94 by 50 feet. The only required equipment in basketball is the ball and two baskets at opposite ends of the court. Basket rims are exactly 10 feet above the ground and 18 inches in diameter. Backboards are ubiquitous though not required; in the NBA, backboards measure 6 by 3½ feet. A rectangular area called a "key" is marked on the court in front of each basket. A foul line is marked at the top of the key, 15 feet from the basket.

An official NBA basketball is round, has eight panels (for grip), has a circumference of 29½ inches, and weighs 22 ounces.

★ **RULES AND TERMINOLOGY:**

Basketball is a beautifully simple sport and the official NBA basketball rulebook is barely half the size of the official baseball and American football rulebooks. The main concepts include:

» *Scoring: Most shots are "field goals" and score 2 points. However a player can score 3 points (a "three-pointer") by successfully shooting from outside an arc measuring 23 feet, 9 inches, from the basket. Players score 1 point when shooting from the foul line.*

» *Violations: The basketball cannot be kicked or struck with a fist. Players in possession of the ball cannot move both feet without dribbling, otherwise they're guilty of a "traveling" violation. Players are guilty of "double dribble" violations if they hold the ball in between dribbles or dribble with two hands. Teams are not allowed to pass or carry the ball into their half of the court once they've advanced the ball into the opponent's half of the court, and must move the ball out of*

TALLEST, SHORTEST, TOP SCORING, AND MOST CONTROVERSIAL
BASKETBALL PLAYERS

★ **TOP 3 TALLEST NBA PLAYERS**
It's a two-way tie for first place. Manute Bol from Sudan and Gheorghe Muresan from Romania top the NBA charts at 7 feet, 7 inches. Bol played for the Washington Bullets (today's Wizards), Golden State Warriors, Miami Heat, and Philadelphia 76ers, Muresan for the Bullets and New Jersey Nets. Despite their height advantage, neither player had a stellar NBA career due to frequent injuries.

Tied for third place are Shawn Bradley and Yao Ming, both 7 feet, 6 inches. Bradley played for Philadelphia and Dallas, Yao for Houston. Yao is a Hall of Fame contender, though his career lasted only eight seasons and was also cut short by injuries.

★ **TOP 3 SHORTEST NBA PLAYERS**
The most famous "little giant" is Tyrone Bogues: at 5 feet, 3 inches, he's the shortest player in NBA history. Bogues had a ten-year career with the Charlotte Hornets and proved that speed and agility matter on the court.

Earl Boykins is the second-shortest NBA player at 5 feet, 5 inches. Boykins never signed a long-term pro contract, but he played numerous journeyman stints for Denver, Golden State, Milwaukee, and Washington.

Anthony Webb's greatest achievements? At 5 feet, 7 inches, Webb miraculously won the NBA's 1986 Slam Dunk Championship. Webb had a twelve-year NBA career and led North Carolina State to the "Sweet 16" round of the NCAA college basketball championships.

★ **TOP 3 NBA SCORERS**
Kareem Abdul-Jabbar, the Los Angeles Lakers' famous forward, had a twenty-year career total of 38,387 points.

Karl Malone, who spent most of his career with the Utah Jazz, had a nineteen-year total of 36,928 points.

Michael Jordan, one of basketball's top players ever, played mainly for the Chicago Bulls and had a fifteen-year total of 32,292 points.

★ **TOP 3 MOST CONTROVERSIAL NBA PLAYERS**
Dennis Rodman. He often acts like he's from a different planet. Rodman's had his issues on and off the court ("As long as I play ball, I can get any woman I want"—too much information, Dennis). But things went haywire for him when he was arrested in 1999 for assaulting his wife, Carmen Electra.

Allen Iverson. Fights, arrests on gun and assault charges, you name it. Iverson is a tough customer, and has the mug shots to prove it.

Tim Hardaway. What more can you say about a player who flat-out hates gay people? "You know, I hate gay people, so I let it be known. I don't like gay people and I don't like to be around gay people. I am homophobic. I don't like it. It shouldn't be in the world or in the United States." No surprise, Hardaway's remarks triggered a media firestorm and ensuing punishment from the NBA.

their half of the court within 10 seconds. Defending players are not allowed to remain inside their own key for more than 3 seconds at a time, unless they're covering an opposing player in possession of the ball.

» **Fouls:** *Referees award fouls against players who illegally interfere with or hinder opposing players. Fouls typically result in a switch of possession. If a foul is committed during the act of shooting, a referee may award a free throw (a penalty shot taken from the foul line). More serious infractions such as fighting or dangerous play earn technical fouls and an automatic chance for the non-offending team to shoot free throws. Individual fouls count against the team foul total in each quarter. In the NBA, if a team exceeds four fouls per quarter, the opposing team is automatically awarded two free throws on all subsequent fouls. Players also have a foul limit: any player who commits six personal fouls in a game is immediately ejected for the remainder of the game (called "fouling out").*

VARIANT » KORFBALL

Korfball was invented by the Dutch in the early 1900s. The game is heavily indebted to basketball and, to a lesser extent, netball. It's one of the few mixed-gender games ever considered for inclusion in the Olympics (korfball was a demonstration sport at the 1920 and '28 Olympics). Two teams of four (two women, two men) shoot a soccer-like ball at a basket suspended 11½ feet high on a pole. Blocking, tackling, and most physical contact are not allowed. Players in possession of the ball are not allowed to dribble, run, or walk with the ball (the netball influence), but instead must pass or shoot.

DODGEBALL

----- LAST MAN STANDING -----

NAYSAYERS WILL CLASSIFY DODGEBALL as a mere game. They have a point: dodgeball is a popular recess activity in many elementary schools. (Believe it or not, the modern schoolyard version of dodgeball has a reputation for bullying and violence, so much so that public schools in New York, New Jersey, Texas, and six other U.S. states have actually banned it completely from school grounds!)

Don't be fooled. Modern dodgeball is played by serious-minded adults in competitive leagues (amateur and pro) both in the USA and internationally. The sport also gained tongue-in-cheek street credibility from the 2004 film *Dodgeball: A True Underdog Story* starring Ben Stiller and Vince Vaughn (not their best work despite grossing $120 million).

★ **BASIC CONCEPT**:

Dodgeball is a team sport. Two sides attempt to eliminate the other by throwing balls (hard!) at opposing players. When a person is hit by a ball they are considered "out." A team wins once all members of the opposing team are eliminated.

There is no limit to the number of players, but teams should start with equal numbers of players. Players are eliminated when hit by a ball that is not caught before touching the ground; or when any part of their body goes beyond the court boundaries, for any reason. If the ball is caught, the thrower is out (in some versions of the game, eliminated players can re-enter the game if another player on their team catches an opponent's thrown ball; in this case the player who threw the ball originally is still out).

★ **EQUIPMENT AND PLAYING SPACE:**

Any basketball or volleyball court—or any large, roughly rectangular outdoor space—will do; there is no "official" size to a dodgeball court, though pro leagues typically use 60-foot by 30-foot indoor volleyball courts as the benchmark. In pro leagues, each half of the dodgeball court is divided in two parts by the attack line, and bounded by the center line and end line. The attack line is typically 8 to 10 feet from the center line and the end line marks the backcourt boundary. Players can only throw balls when standing between the end and attack lines. The rest of the court is considered neutral territory.

There's no official ball size, nor any limit to the number of balls used simultaneously in a game (six is a common number). Padded balls work best, either volleyballs or large handballs.

★ **WHERE TO PLAY AND WATCH:**

The National Amateur Dodgeball Association (NADA; www.dodge ballusa.com) organizes neighborhood teams and tournaments across the USA. The National Dodgeball League (NDL; www.thendl.com) is the umbrella organization for the USA's current eighteen professional teams (Oregon Avalanche, Boston Undertakers, Pittsburgh Punishers—you get the idea). The annual NDL Dodgeball World Championship draws teams from Denmark, New Zealand, Australia, Canada, and most U.S. states.

5 TIPS FOR DODGEBALL NEWBIES

★ *Always aim low. This makes your balls harder to catch and ensures you'll never throw an errant head shot.*

★ *It sounds obvious but, please, throw from the front of the court and stand at the back when not throwing.*

★ *Throw together—if your team holds more than one ball, throw them at the same target at the same time. Dodging one ball is hard enough; dodging three balls is nearly impossible.*

★ *It's called "dodge" ball for a reason. Learning to dodge the ball effectively can make you just as useful as players with quick strong throws.*

★ *Women: Don't get pummeled by a bunch of angry dodgeball-wielding dudes. Plenty of neighborhood leagues offer women-only teams.*

FOUR SQUARE

FOUR SQUARE STARTED—AND STILL THRIVES—on school playgrounds. It's popular because it blends aggressive physicality (hit the ball as hard as you can!) with straightforward gameplay. It's also a deeply social sport: players can choose to band together to eliminate mutual threats and, by knocking out competition, they move up in the world. Think of "king of the hill" minus the hill.

★ **BASIC CONCEPT:**

Four players stand alone in the quadrants of a square labeled from 1 to 4 (4 is highest, 1 is lowest). The player in square 4 serves the ball to square 1. The ball is then bounced from square to square until the ball is hit out of bounds (hitter is out) or the receiver cannot hit or deflect the ball into another square on one bounce (receiver is out). Eliminated players leave the court, all players advance to fill empty squares, and a new player joins at the lowest-ranked square (square 1). In tournament play the goal is to gain points by advancing to square 4 and retaining serve.

★ **EQUIPMENT AND PLAYING SPACE:**

Four players, one rubber ball, and a piece of chalk—it doesn't get much simpler than four square. Use any soft bouncy ball (the "official" ball is an 8½-inch rubber playground ball inflated to two pounds) and draw a large square divided into quadrants (leagues start with 20-foot by 20-foot or 16-foot by 16-foot squares).

FOUR SQUARE 4EVR

ACCORDING TO WIKIPEDIA, the world's longest game of four square was played in 2011 by fifteen students at Indiana's Manchester College. The match lasted thirty hours.

★ **RULES AND TERMINOLOGY:**

Squares 4 and 1 are always positioned diagonally from each other, and square 4 always serves to square 1. The server must drop the ball and serve from the bounce, and the ball must bounce once in the receiving square. The service receiver then hits the ball to either square 2 or 3 (not back to square 4). After the service receiver touches the ball, the ball is considered in play.

Players are eliminated by failing to hit the ball into another square, hitting the ball out of turn, hitting the ball out of bounds (the external outlines of the larger square), or for holding, catching, or carrying the ball. Players in squares 4 and 3 often form a temporary alliance and set each other up with easy high-bounce passes that can be fired hard and fast at opponents.

HANDBALL

----- A PERFECT BLEND OF ICE HOCKEY AND BASKETBALL -----

HANDBALL, THE TEAM VERSION, is an Olympic sport and has been since the 1972 games in Munich (it's also played at the Pan American and Asian Games). This makes handball yet another professional sport with a playground pedigree . . . though you would hardly recognize the modern game if your last handball experience was at recess in third grade.

Handball's popularity beyond the schoolyard stems, in part, from the game's relative antiquity. A version of handball was played in medieval France. The game was officially codified in northern Europe in the 1890s, and if you're looking for the birthplace of the modern game, give due credit to Denmark. A version of the game—called field handball—was played at the 1936 Olympics. The International Handball Federation (IHF, www.ihf.info) organized world championships starting from 1938, which nowadays are typically dominated by teams from Germany, Russia, and France.

★ **BASIC CONCEPT:**

The Olympic version of handball, called team handball, features two teams of seven players (one goalie, six fielders) attempting to pass and throw a small ball into the opponent's goal. The team with the highest score after two 30-minute halves wins.

Handball teams move the ball up and down the court in a fashion similar to basketball: after receiving the ball, handball players can only hold it for 3 seconds before passing, dribbling, or shooting.

As in ice hockey, defensive handball players are allowed some physical contact to prevent an attacker from scoring. Also like ice hockey, there's a large crease surrounding each goal that is off-limits to all players except the defending goalies. Referees award free throws and penalties (noted with yellow and red cards) for infractions. An infraction that prevents a clear shot on goal results in a penalty shot.

★ **EQUIPMENT AND PLAYING SPACE:**

The official team handball court measures 40 meters by 20 meters, with goals on either end measuring 3 meters by 2 meters (smaller than soccer goals, much larger than ice hockey goals). The crease surrounding each goal is made of two quarter-circles with a 6-meter radius, connected by a line parallel to the goal.

Handballs are intentionally small and meant to fit comfortably in your hand. Official size varies based on the age and sex of the players; the Olympic men's teams use a 60-centimeter ball (volleyballs are 65–67 centimeters, for comparison).

★ **RULES AND TERMINOLOGY:**

Players can touch the ball with any part of the body above and including the knee. Goalies inside the crease can touch the ball with all parts of the body (including their feet). Players in control of the ball have just three options—shoot, pass, or dribble—and can stand still for no more than 3 seconds.

The crease is off-limits to all players except the defending goalie. That said, as long as players start a jump from outside the crease, they can legally catch balls in the air and shoot or pass in a single motion before landing in the crease. Cool! Once in the crease players must take the most direct path out or face a turnover penalty.

Matches at the professional level are divided into two 30-minute periods/halves. In case of ties, two 5-minute overtimes and, if necessary, a best-of-five penalty shootout determine the game winner.

A BRIEF HISTORY OF HANDBALL

Traditional handball was brought to the USA in the nineteenth century by Irish immigrants, and the game has strong United Kingdom and Irish lineages. The oldest recorded mention of a game involving a ball struck with a bare hand dates from 1427 in Scotland (apparently King James I requested a palace wall to be filled in, to improve the playing surface). There's also a written mention of handball from sixteenth-century Ireland.

★ **WHERE TO PLAY AND WATCH:**

The Olympics are an obvious choice. If you can't wait that long for a match, the International Handball Federation sponsors world championships every two years (in odd years) for both men and women.

VARIANT » TRADITIONAL (AMERICAN) HANDBALL

American handball is the traditional playground version. All that's required is a sturdy flat wall, a small rubber ball, and two players keen to smack the ball with fists or bare hands.

Games are usually played head-to-head or by two teams of two players. Courts have four walls, three walls, or one wall. In all cases the ball is served by dropping it to the floor and hitting it with your hand or fist on the bounce. The ball must hit the front wall first (and, in three- and four-wall versions, can hit at most one additional side wall). The returning player must hit the ball back to the front wall before the ball bounces off the floor a second time.

Games are typically played to 21 points and only the server can score. It's a definite no-no for players to block their opponents from hitting the ball—in competitive play, blocking results in an immediate switch of servers.

The ball itself is usually a racquetball (small and bouncy) or purpose-made handball (small, hard, and less bouncy). On playgrounds you'll want one of those large, red rubber balls.

KICKBALL

----- BASEBALL WITHOUT BATS -----

KICKBALL IS CURRENTLY TRENDY WITH THE HIPSTER CROWD on playgrounds across America. Dozens of amateur and neighborhood leagues have sprouted up since the late 1990s. Kickball is simple to play and easy to learn given its close kinship with baseball. And it is eminently social: teams promote drinkathons and postgame meet-ups as part of kickball's appeal.

As sports go, kickball is not the pinnacle of athleticism. Don't look for it in the Olympics anytime soon.

★ BASIC CONCEPT:

Kickball is played almost exactly like baseball and softball. Two teams compete to score points by running between and touching four bases (in order!) without getting thrown out. The glaring difference is that bats are not used. Instead, pitchers roll a rubber ball towards the catcher, and a "batter" or kicker attempts to kick the ball into play.

As in baseball, the ideal kickball team has nine players: pitcher, catcher, three basemen, three outfielders, and one shortstop. Many leagues require at least one or two members of the opposite sex on each team. Kickball games typically last five or six innings.

★ EQUIPMENT AND PLAYING SPACE:

You can use any standard baseball or softball diamond. All you really need are four bases (first through third plus home plate) and a round rubber ball (typically 8½ to 10 inches in diameter).

★ RULES AND TERMINOLOGY:

Refer to the baseball section of this book for the basic rules of kickball. The main differences between baseball and kickball are:

> » **Pitching:** *Pitchers have lots of latitude when throwing. The only requirements are: before reaching home plate the ball must bounce at least twice or roll on the ground; the ball must cross home plate; and the ball cannot bounce higher than one foot as it crosses home plate.*

> » **Kicking:** *Players can use any part of the leg, below the knee, to kick the ball. Players cannot kick the ball before it reaches home plate (doing so results in a strike). Players are out after three strikes or four fouls (note: fouls never count as strikes). A foul is any ball that lands or rolls out of play, is kicked above the knee or touched twice by the kicker, or is kicked from outside the regulation "batter's box."*

» **Bunting:** *Some leagues allow bunting, some do not. In the former, a ball is in play as long as it does not go outside the "foul lines" running between home plate and first and third bases. In the latter, a ball must also go past the pitching mound or else it is considered foul.*

» **Tagging:** *Unlike baseball, in kickball it is allowed (completely encouraged!) to throw the ball at a runner in an attempt to get them out. This is in addition to tagging the runner out at a base. The only restriction is you cannot aim at the runner's head.*

» **Base Running:** *Runners are not allowed to lead off the bases. A runner who is caught doing so is out.*

» **Double Plays:** *When a defensive player catches a ball, they can throw to the mound for a double play. If the pitcher catches the ball* before *the lead base runner returns to their original base, the lead runner is out (any other base runners are deemed safe).*

★ **WHERE TO PLAY AND WATCH:**

The World Adult Kickball Association (WAKA; www.kickball.com) sponsors an annual Founders Cup Tournament World Kickball Championship in Las Vegas, Nevada. The National Kickball Association (NKA; www.nka-kc.com) hosts a less formal tournament annually in Louisville, Kentucky. If you're keen to play yourself, both organizations sponsor leagues around the country.

NETBALL

WORLDWIDE MORE THAN TWENTY MILLION PEOPLE play netball. Which makes netball (for Americans, at least) one of the most famous sports they've never heard of. This is highly ironic, given that netball was created in America, by Americans, specifically to be a less physical version of the iconic American sport of basketball.

The two sports—basketball and netball—were invented days apart in 1891 at the very same school in Massachusetts. Basketball was intended as a sport for men. Netball was—and still is—a sport primarily for women. The game traveled to England in the early twentieth century and became hugely popular with school-age girls throughout the British Commonwealth, in particular Australia, New Zealand, South Africa, Sri Lanka, India, and the West Indies.

In 1995 netball became an Olympic "recognized sport" (i.e., formally recognized by the International Olympic Committee). It has yet to be played at a summer Olympics. Instead, tune into the World Netball Championships held every four years and sponsored by the sport's global governing body, the International Federation of Netball Associations (IFNA; www.netball.org).

★ **BASIC CONCEPT:**

In netball two teams of seven compete to score as many points as possible (and to prevent the opposing team from scoring). Goals are made by shooting a ball through a basket (called a "goal ring") anchored atop a 10-foot pole. Unlike basketball, in netball there are no backboards behind the nets.

Netball players are assigned specific positions that restrict their movements on court (players display position on their game jerseys, along with their name or number). Players in possession of the ball cannot take more than one step before passing it, and they must pass the ball or shoot for a goal within three seconds. Dribbling is not allowed. And unlike basketball, only designated shooting players (two per team) can score goals. All other players have specific non-shooting roles.

Netball games typically last 60 minutes and are divided into 15-minute quarters. The team with more goals wins the game.

AUSSIE! AUSSIE! AUSSIE!

THE AUSTRALIANS HAVE WON TEN TITLES—and have thoroughly dominated international netball—since the first World Netball Championships were held in 1963. New Zealand is a powerhouse, too, winning four titles and giving Australia plenty to worry about in the run-up to the 2015 World Championships in Sydney.

Netball courts measure 100 feet by 50 feet (slightly larger than NBA 94-foot-by-50-foot basketball courts) and are divided into thirds: a "goal third" at either end surrounding a "center third" in the middle. The goal rings are surrounded by a 16-foot semicircle, called a "shooting circle."

The typical netball is made of rubber or leather, weighs 14 to 16 ounces, and has a circumference of 27 to 28 inches. A size 5 soccer ball (football) is commonly used.

★ **RULES AND TERMINOLOGY:**

Refer to the basketball section of this book for the basic rules of netball. The main differences between netball and basketball are:

> » *No contact is allowed between players, either accidentally or deliberately. Netball is a no-contact sport.*

> » *As such, a defending player must maintain a distance of 3 feet from an attacking player with the ball.*

> » *A player may catch the ball with one or both hands and must pass it—or shoot for goal—within 3 seconds. There is no dribbling, and once a player catches the ball only one step may be taken.*

> » *There are seven predefined positions in netball, governing where and how individual players can move on the court. The defensive positions are goal keeper, goal defense, and wing defense. A center coordinates ball movement between the defensive and attacking thirds of the court. The attacking positions are wing attack, goal attack, and goal shooter.*

> » *Only two positions on the court can shoot (goal attack and goal shooter) and shots can only be taken from within the opposing team's shooting circle.*

The main difference here is that the indoor court is surrounded by a net on all sides, including the ceiling. This prevents the ball from ever leaving the court, making indoor netball a brutally fast-paced and exhausting version of the main sport. To compensate, the game is shortened to two 15-minute halves.

In seven-a-side games the rules are essentially unchanged.

Positions are streamlined in six-a-side matches with just two attackers, two centers, and two defenders per team. Attacking and defending players can move anywhere in their half of the court, including the shooting circle. Centers are allowed the reverse: play the whole court except the shooting circles.

The five-a-side version features two attackers, two defenders, and a center per team. All positions can move anywhere on the entire court except the shooting circles, which are reserved for the respective defenders and attackers.

TETHERBALL

----- WRAP A BALL AROUND A POLE -----

IS IT A GAME OR A SPORT? That's a fair question given that tetherball is played mostly in schools.

On the other hand tetherball does have a governing body. The World Tetherball Association (www.worldtetherballassociation.com), and it meets—and exceeds, to be honest—the pure definition of "sport." Tetherball is highly competitive and requires physical prowess as well as mental acumen. Nobody expects to see tetherball at the summer Olympics, but surely the sporting pantheon has ample room for a modest sport such as tetherball.

★ **BASIC CONCEPT:**

A rope is used to attach a ball to the top of a pole, and two players compete to hit the ball repeatedly in one direction until the rope wraps completely around the pole.

★ **EQUIPMENT AND PLAYING SPACE:**

The traditional tetherball pole is 10 feet tall. Tetherball ropes are typically 8 feet long and attached to the top of the pole at one end, with a volleyball or other similar-size ball at the other end. Tetherballs are attached to the rope via a loop fastener protruding from, or via a fastener recessed below, the ball's surface.

★ **RULES AND TERMINOLOGY:**

The server can hit the ball in either direction with any part of the hand or arm (below the elbow). Once in play, the opposing player attempts to hit the ball in the opposite direction.

Players must stay in their half of the court (a line divides the court into halves). If a player's foot crosses the line, an offside penalty is awarded. Other penalties or fouls include touching the rope; double-hitting the ball (it's okay to hit the ball simultaneously with two hands, but the touches must be truly simultaneous); carrying, pushing, or lifting the ball; and touching the pole. All penalties or fouls incur the same result: play is halted, the ball is returned to the point where it was wrapped when the violation occurred, and the non-offending player serves.

A game is won when the rope is completely wrapped around the pole.

Tetherball matches are often played best of five or best of seven, with the winner needing to win by a margin of two games or more.

Tetherball is all about the serve, and experienced players know to serve the ball so that it flies out of reach over their opponent's head. This is easier said than done. Defensive players should move constantly around their half of the court to counter the dreaded over-the-head shot from their opponent.

VARIANT » SWINGBALL

This version of the game dominates in Europe and Australia. The key differences are the ball (tennis ball instead of a volleyball) and the use of racquets (preferably plastic paddles, though any racquet can be substituted in a pinch) instead of hands for hitting. All other rules are identical. Not to sound like your mother, but eye protection is de rigueur in swingball.

ULTIMATE

----- SOCCER MEETS FOOTBALL, WITH A FLYING DISC -----

ULTIMATE COMBINES THE NONSTOP ACTION OF SOCCER with the passing skills of American football. Ultimate is a no-contact sport, and the pace is grueling. Two teams compete to score goals in the opponent's end zone. Turnovers are frequent in Ultimate unlike in football, leading to quick transitions from offense to defense and back again.

Ultimate is not an Olympic sport (yet!), though it is played in more than forty countries and is featured in major international sporting competitions. The sport's main governing body, the World Flying Disc Federation (WFDF; www.wfdf.org), organizes annual championships in every region of the globe, in multiple categories: traditional Ultimate, beach (Ultimate on sand), guts (two teams face off across a neutral zone, scoring points when the opposing team can't catch a legal throw), and freestyle (teams compete with choreographed routines of throws, catches, and fancy moves).

In the United States, where more than 4.5 million people play each year, Ultimate is making the jump from amateur competition to major-league sport. An eight-team professional league kicked off its inaugural season in 2012 under the auspices of the American Ultimate Disc League (AUDL; www.theaudl.com).

★ BASIC CONCEPT:

Ultimate is played by two teams of seven players, on a rectangular field 64 meters long by 37 meters wide plus two end zones (each 18 meters deep). The goal of the game is to score points by catching a pass in the opponent's end zone (worth one point). Official games are played to 15 points.

Players move the disc up the field by throwing it to teammates. Players must stop moving while in possession of the disc, but can pivot and pass (in any direction) to any other receiver. Turnovers are frequent and happen when a pass is dropped, blocked, or intercepted; the disc is thrown out of bounds; or when a player holds the disc for more than 10 seconds.

★ RULES AND TERMINOLOGY:

No physical contact is allowed between players (picks and screens are also prohibited). All physical contact results in a foul, which usually means the perpetrator loses possession. Unlike nearly all major sports, Ultimate does not have referees and instead relies on self-refereeing and group dispute resolution. As naive as it may sound to new players, Ultimate is governed by a "spirit of the game" philosophy that stresses sportsmanship and fair play.

VARIANT » DISC GOLF

Disc golf is just like it sounds: golf, but with a Frisbee-like throwing disc instead of a club and ball. Like Ultimate, disc golf is highly competitive. The idea is to throw a disc into a basket or target in the fewest number of throws possible. Disc golf courses are just like standard golf courses. Both have nine or eighteen holes and each hole has a par (the average number of throws it takes to get the disc to its target).

A ROSE BY ANY OTHER NAME

THE SPORT USED TO BE CALLED ULTIMATE FRISBEE until the lawyers got involved. Frisbee is a registered trademark of the Wham-O toy company, so the word was dropped by the sport's governing bodies. Wisely, the governing bodies did not rebrand the sport as "Ultimate Flying Disc" but instead kept the name short and sweet: Ultimate.

VOLLEYBALL

HOW'S THIS FOR BRAGGING RIGHTS? The state of Massachusetts was the birthplace of *two* iconic American sports: basketball in 1891 and volleyball in 1895. The latter was the brainchild of William Morgan, who worked at a local YMCA. Morgan's original game was a blend of tennis and handball, intended as a less physical pastime than the new and rougher game of basketball.

The sport quickly caught on, spreading throughout the Americas and overseas thanks in no small part to more than 15,000 volleyballs shipped by the U.S. War Department to American troops stationed in places such as Cuba, the Philippines, and China. In the United States itself volleyball was added to grammar school and collegiate sports programs, in large part through the lobbying efforts of the YMCA.

By 1920 the set and spike were introduced and the "three hits" rule was codified in the sport's rulebook. In 1928 the U.S. Volleyball Association (now USA Volleyball; www.usavolleyball.org) was formed, followed in 1947 by the Fédération Internationale de Volleyball (FIVB; www.fivb.org). The first Volleyball World Championships were held in 1949 (men) and 1952 (women), followed by volleyball's debut as an Olympic sport at the 1964 Tokyo games. In 1969 the National Collegiate Athletic Association (NCAA) added volleyball to its list of sanctioned sports.

★ **BASIC CONCEPT:**

Indoor volleyball is played by two six-player teams on a rectangular court divided in half by a net. The serving team hits the ball over the net into the opponent's half of the court, and the receiving team attempts to return the ball without the ball touching the ground.

Once the ball is in play each side is allowed three hits, or touches, before returning the ball over the net. Generally the first two touches are used to set up an attacking player's delivery of an impossible-to-return "kill shot" to the opposing team.

The team that wins the point earns the right to serve. Traditionally only the serving team could score points and individual sets were won by the first team to score 15 total points (and be 2 points ahead). However, in 2000 the FIVB switched from so-called "side-out scoring" to a new "rally point" system, whereby sets are played to 25 points each and either team can score (regardless of who is serving).

Official volleyball matches are best-of-five sets with the fifth set (when necessary) played to 15 points.

IS VOLLEYBALL REALLY THAT POPULAR?

AN ESTIMATED 46 MILLION AMERICANS PLAY VOLLEYBALL, and more than 800 million people worldwide play volleyball at least once a week. After soccer, volleyball is the world's second most played sport.

Volleyball courts are 18 meters long and 9 meters wide, divided equally by a 1-meter-tall net. The top of the net must hang approximately 2.4 meters above the court (slightly less high for women).

Each half of the court is subdivided by an "attack line" that is 3 meters from the net, creating "front court" and "back court" areas. The entire

court is surrounded by a "free zone" measuring at least 3 meters wide and used to mark the boundaries within which players can stray without being considered out of bounds.

Official volleyballs must be 65 to 67 centimeters in circumference and weigh 260 to 280 grams.

Volleyball is a heavily regulated sport—USA volleyball's official rule book is more than two hundred pages long! The critical concepts include:

> » ***Serving:*** *The serving player must begin outside their own backcourt line. Servers cannot cross into the court until the ball is hit. Servers can strike the ball in many different ways, including underhand (striking the ball while holding it below the waist), overhand (tossing the ball into the air before striking), and the jump serve (an overhand serve thrown high into the air, with the server then jumping to strike the ball from an elevated position).*

> » ***Hitting the Ball:*** *Players can legally strike the ball with any part of their body, though usually the hands and forearms are preferred. A ball is considered in bounds if any part of it touches a side or end line. Players can strike the ball in the free zone, too, as long as the ball crosses the side or end lines in the air.*

» **Pass, Set, Spike:** *These are the most common types of volley-ball shots. A "pass" is when a player makes first contact with an incoming ball and redirects it (using either the fingertips or forearms) to the setter. The "set" is usually the second touch, intended to deliver an easy-to-handle ball to the attacker. The "spike" is the third and final touch made by an attacker, ideally hit so that the ball rockets into the opponent's court and becomes nonreturnable.*

» **Blocks and Digs:** *A block is when players stand at the net and jump to block an incoming ball at (or ideally before it crosses) the net. A blocking player (or players) can cross above the net as long as they don't actually touch the net or cross the invisible line underneath the net. A dig refers to rescuing a spike or other attack shot from hitting the ground. Digs are often last-gasp lunges, as the defending player desperately tries to prevent the ball from hitting the ground.*

» **Scoring:** *Teams score a point, whether they served or not, whenever the ball makes floor contact on their opponent's side of the court; the opposing team hits the ball out of bounds; or the opposing team makes a foul.*

» **Common Faults:** *The most common faults are failing to return the ball over the net within the allotted three touches (not including a block); hitting the ball out of bounds; hitting the ball consecutively by the same player; throwing, lifting, or catching the ball by any player; or touching the net during play.*

» **Player Rotation:** *Teams are required to field three players in the front court and three in the back court. When a team wins the serve, all six players must rotate their positions clockwise. The previous server moves one space over in the back court, one of the back court players moves to the front court, and one of the front court players moves to the serving position. Players are not required to maintain their positions once the* *ball is in play; instead, the rotation governs where players start as the ball is served.*

» **The Libero:** *This is a new position, introduced by the FIVB in 1998 to (theoretically) foster more digs and rallies. The libero is a defensive specialist who cannot touch the ball when it is entirely above the net. The libero is also not allowed to serve. On the plus side, the libero is not required to rotate positions, but instead can roam the court. On offense the libero's role is to pass the ball to teammates; on defense the libero's role is to dig, dig, dig!*

VARIANT » BEACH VOLLEYBALL

Beach volleyball is not a mere a spinoff of indoor volleyball. Sure, indoor volleyball is the older and more established sport. Yet since the first official game of beach volleyball was played in Santa Monica, California, back in 1947, the sport has grown by leaps and bounds and has become a major sport in its own right.

Beach volleyball in the Olympics? Yes, since Atlanta in 1996.

Beach volleyball with international and national governing bodies? Absolutely.

The FIVB knows a good marketing angle when it sees one, and has embraced beach volleyball from the very beginning. When it comes to television popularity and advertising sponsorships, beach volleyball wins hands-down over indoor volleyball. After all, who doesn't like watching tan, swimsuit-clad athletes run and jump in the sand??

The main differences between the two sports are the playing surfaces (a smaller sand court versus a larger hard-surface indoor court), the number of players (beach volleyball teams are limited to two players a side), and the, uh, uniforms (in 1999 the FIVB required both men and women to wear only swimsuits—plus an optional hat, thanks very much).

Some of the rules differ, too. In beach volleyball players are not required to rotate. And the rules on double-hitting are stricter (mainly because beach volleyballs are slightly larger and tacky, to make them less slick and bouncy in outdoor weather conditions). Scoring is unique, with sets played to 21 points and matches won by the team that wins two sets (third sets, when necessary, are played to 15 points).

Beach volleyball also uses a system of "signaling" that does not exist in indoor volleyball. Beach players communicate with each other using elaborate hand signals, hidden from their opponents' view. Signals are given prior to the serve to indicate what type of block to use against the return attack from the opposing team.

One reason for the popularity of beach volleyball is the game's accessibility. Frequent amateur and pro matches are held year-round, in popular beach destinations around the world. Check the USA Volleyball and FIVB Web sites for current dates.

03

Baseball

CHAPTER THREE

MAJOR LEAGUE BASEBALL

----- "IT AIN'T OVER TILL IT'S OVER." -----
—*YOGI BERRA*

BASEBALL HAS BEEN AMERICA'S NATIONAL PASTIME since at least the 1830s—though most Americans would be surprised at how different the modern game is from its nineteenth-century predecessor.

One reason the sport is so deeply ingrained in the American psyche is that baseball's history often mirrors the history of the country at large. Racial discrimination and baseball's black-only "negro leagues," tensions between management and unions, urban flight and the rise of West Coast franchises, the concentration of wealth by elite players and owners—at so many points in American history, baseball has reflected the warts-and-all face of America itself.

Each time baseball suffers a setback—and there have been many, from the thrown 1919 World Series to players' strikes in 1972, '81, '85 and '94, to the Mark McGwire and Barry Bonds steroid scandals—something happens on the field to rekindle the passion of its fans (a nail-biting playoff race, an epic championship series, or perhaps a team breaking a self-declared curse and winning a World Series for the first time in decades). This unpredictability, coupled with the sport's ability to reflect the best and worst of its times, is what makes baseball America's much loved, and often criticized, national pastime.

7 FAMOUS HOME RUN CALLS

★ *"Hey, hey!"* —JACK BRICKHOUSE

★ *"Forget it."* —VIN SCULLY

★ *"It could be, it might be, it is! A home run!"*
 —HARRY CARAY

★ *"How about that?"* —MEL ALLEN

★ *"Back, back, back, back . . . gone!"* —CHRIS BERMAN

★ *"You can put it on the board . . . Yessssssss!"*
 —KEN HARRELSON

★ *"Get out the rye bread and mustard, grandma,
 it's grand salami time!"*
 —DAVE NIEHAUS (CALLING A GRAND SLAM HOME RUN)

★ ★ ★ ★ ★ ············· U.B.S. ············· ★ ★ ★ ★ ★ ★
MAJOR LEAGUE BASEBALL

While baseball is quintessentially an American sport, it is also played professionally in more than a dozen countries from Japan and Australia to South Korea and Venezuela. Baseball was even a full-medal sport at the Olympics from 1992 to 2008, attesting to the sport's growing international appeal.

Historically speaking, the idea that Abner Doubleday invented baseball in Cooperstown, New York, in 1839 has been repeatedly proven a myth: it's a lovely story, but it never happened. Instead the history of baseball is more complicated. It originated in England as the game of rounders, which is a hybrid of modern baseball and cricket, with a little softball thrown in for good measure. Rounders made its way to North America in the eighteenth century and at some point morphed into baseball. By the 1830s baseball was played in back lots and empty fields across the United States, under rules that would be largely unrecognizable today. Back then it was okay to throw the ball *at* a runner for an out, pitching was underhanded, and balls caught on one bounce were out.

Pretty much everybody agrees the first official game of baseball took place on June 19, 1846, in Hoboken, New Jersey. The score at the end of the four-inning game? The New York Nine defeated the New York Knickerbockers 23 to 1. In 1869 the first truly professional baseball team, the Cincinnati Red Stockings, was formed. The National League followed seven years later, followed by the American League in 1901 and the very first World Series in 1903 (won by the American League's Boston Americans, later renamed the Boston Red Sox).

★   **BASIC CONCEPT**:

Two teams of nine players alternate between batting and fielding in an attempt to score runs. Batters try to hit a thrown ball with a bat and, if successful, complete a circuit around four bases (first base, second base, third base, home plate). One run is earned for returning

TOP 10 ALL-TIME HOME RUN HITTERS

* *Barry Bonds: 762*

* *Hank Aaron: 755*

* *Babe Ruth: 714*

* *Willie Mays: 660*

* *Ken Griffey, Jr.: 630*

* *Alex Rodriguez: 629 (still playing)*

* *Sammy Sosa: 609*

* *Jim Thome: 604 (still playing)*

* *Frank Robinson: 586*

* *Mark McGwire: 583*

safely to home plate. The fielding team tries to stop the batting team from scoring by recording "outs" in a variety of ways: catching a hit ball prior to the bounce, tagging a base runner before he successfully reaches the next base in rotation, or striking out the batter.

The teams switch from batting to fielding after every three outs (a half-inning). Professional games are divided into nine innings, and in each inning the teams both bat once. The higher score wins at the end of the game (baseball does not allow ties, so games continue until a winner is decided, even if that requires many more innings than the official nine).

★ EQUIPMENT AND PLAYING SPACE:

Every professional baseball field is different and features its own architectural quirks. That said, there are basic requirements for baseball fields: two foul lines must extend forward from home plate at 45-degree angles, and the 90-degree area within the foul lines is considered fair territory. Four bases are arranged in a diamond shape and set 90 feet apart. A slightly elevated pitcher's mound is set 60½ feet from home plate and features a rectangular rubber plate (the "rubber") used by pitchers to anchor their back throwing foot. The distance from home plate to the outfield fences varies at every park, from 390 to 435 feet measured at center field.

Batters swing with a tapered, wooden bat that measures no more than 2.61 inches in diameter at the thicker hitting end. Bats have a maximum legal length of 42 inches.

Baseballs are hard, round balls with 9-inch circumferences. Professional balls have a rubber or cork center (to improve hitting velocities), a leather covering, and feature traditional stitching for better grip when pitching and throwing. The only other required gear is a baseball glove, used by fielding teams to catch balls; and a batting helmet to protect the batter's head.

★ RULES AND TERMINOLOGY:

Baseball is a sport of statistics and rules. Statistics cover elements such as batting average (hits divided by appearances at bat, expressed as a three-digit percentage), walks, runs batted in, earned runs (for pitchers—the number of runs that did not occur as a result of errors or dropped balls by a catcher), shutouts, strikeouts, saves—if you can imagine it, baseball likely has a statistic for it.

The official baseball rulebook is a mind-numbing 130 pages long, governing everything from pitchers touching their lips (not allowed on the pitcher's plate) to the style of players' shirts (slit sleeves are a no-no). Needless to say, the following are merely some important concepts in the massive tome that is baseball's rulebook.

» **Batting:** *Batters stand at home plate and face the opposing pitcher, who delivers a pitch at speeds up to 105 miles per hour. Every batter has a personal "strike zone" extending above home plate between the batter's knees and the midpoint between the top of a batter's uniform pants and the top of the shoulders. It's a strike when batters fail to hit balls pitched in the strike zone. It's also a strike when the batter hits a ball into foul territory. Batters are allowed three strikes before they are called out (one exception: batters cannot be called out for hitting balls into foul territory; the count continues to stand at two strikes). If a batter decides not to swing at a ball pitched outside the strike zone, it's a called a "ball." Pitchers are allowed four balls before being penalized by having the batter automatically sent to first base (called a "walk" or "base on balls"). If the batter is hit by a pitch at any point, the batter is automatically awarded first base.*

» **Hitting and Scoring:** *When a batter hits the ball into play, either from a full swing or from a gentle tap called a bunt, he must drop the bat and run towards first base. It's called a single if he reaches first base safely on a hit, a double for reaching second base, and a triple for reaching third base. It's a home run if the ball is hit within fair territory and over the outfield boundary or fences; the batter plus any runners on base are given a free pass of the bases, with one run scoring for every player who reaches home plate. One of the most beautiful hits in baseball is a grand slam: a home run made with the bases loaded, thereby scoring four total runs.*

» **Base Running:** *Base runners attempt to advance any time the ball is legally put into play (runners on second and third base aren't required to advance, however a runner on first base must attempt to advance when a ball lands in fair territory).*

7 FAMOUS BASEBALL QUOTES

★ "Baseball is ninety percent mental, the other half is physical." —YOGI BERRA

★ "Baseball has been good to me since I quit trying to play it." —WHITEY HERZOG

★ "There are three things you can do in a baseball game. You can win, or you can lose, or it can rain." —CASEY STENGEL

★ "Baseball is the only field of endeavor where a man can succeed three times out of ten and be considered a good performer." —TED WILLIAMS

★ "Baseball is like church. Many attend but few understand." —WES WESTRUM

★ "I watch a lot of baseball on the radio." —GERALD FORD

★ "I'd walk through hell in a gasoline suit to play baseball." —PETE ROSE

Runners must return to their original bases when a ball rolls foul inside the infield. When a ball is caught prior to a bounce, the batter is out (called a fly out) but any base runners can attempt to advance as long as they "tag up" from their starting base and then run only once the ball is caught. Runners can also attempt to "steal a base" by running to the next base once the pitcher has begun his pitching motion.

» ***Pitching:*** *It's common for multiple pitchers to play in a single game. There is no limit on the number of pitchers, which leads to specialization (starting pitcher, relief pitcher, closer, left-handed specialist, etc.). Once a pitcher begins his pitching motion, he is required to complete the motion (otherwise he's called for a balking penalty, which sends the batter to first base). Pitchers are required to use one of two standard pitching positions (windup or the set) and cannot do anything to affect the aerodynamics of the ball (it's illegal to spit on the ball, rub the ball, or alter the ball in any way). Most pitchers alternate between two or three of the most common pitch types including the curveball (the ball dives down as it nears the plate), slider (similar to a curveball, but thrown faster), or fastball (hard and fast at the plate).*

★ **WHERE TO PLAY AND WATCH:**

Major League Baseball (MLB; www.mlb.com) is the United States' professional league and the de facto governing body for baseball when it comes to setting rules. The highlight of the MLB baseball calendar is the annual World Series held in October.

The International Baseball Federation (IBAF; www.ibaf.org) is the sport's international organizing body. It was formerly responsible for baseball's two largest championships outside the World Series: the Baseball World Cup (first played in 1938) and the World Baseball Classic (inaugurated in 2006). The former tournament was discontinued in 2011 in favor of an expanded World Baseball Classic, to be held every four years starting from 2013. The World Baseball Classic features professional players from major leagues around the world and is the only international tournament sanctioned by Major League Baseball. Teams from Japan have so far dominated the 16-nation field of competitors (the United States national team earned fourth place in 2009).

ROUNDERS

----- THE ORIGINAL SPORT OF BASEBALL -----

THINK "BASEBALL" WITH SPLASHES OF CRICKET and softball thrown in. Rounders is an ancient game, dating back to at least the 1650s in England. The basic idea is that a small hard ball is bowled (what Americans would call pitched) underhand to a batter, who tries to hit the ball using a baseball-style bat. Players score by running a circuit of four bases, each marked with a stick or post labeled first post, second post, third post, fourth post. If the batter reaches the second or third post in one hit, the batting team scores one half-rounder. If the batter reaches fourth post in one hit, the batting team scores one rounder.

If batters stop at a post, they must maintain contact with the post with either the hand or bat. Otherwise the fielding team can "stump" (touch with the ball) the following post to put them out. Players are also out if a fielder catches the ball prior to a bounce; if a batter reaches a base that has been stumped; or if the batter drops the bat while running the bases (like in cricket, the bat must be carried by the runner).

Like baseball, rounders is divided into innings (two innings is the traditional game length) and played by two teams of nine. Rounders is still played in England and Ireland, especially in grade schools.

Boating and Rowing

CHAPTER FOUR

DRAGON BOAT RACING

DRAGON BOAT RACING STARTED IN SOUTH-CENTRAL CHINA more than 2,500 years ago. Part competitive pursuit and part religious ceremony, dragon boat racing honors the ancient Chinese dragon deity and is meant to ensure rainfall for rice crops and prosperity for rice farmers.

Dragon boat races feature prominently in celebrations of Duanwu, a festival held each year on the fifth day of the fifth month of the lunar calendar (typically in June). Since the mid-1970s dragon boat racing has grown into a popular international sport, with dragon boat teams paddling competitively in Chinese communities from Hong Kong to California, Europe to southeast Asia. At the 2011 World Dragon Boat Racing Championship held in Tampa, Florida, teams from more than seventy countries competed!

★ **BASIC CONCEPT:**

Dragon boats are human-powered canoes traditionally made from hollowed-out logs. The standard boat is 12 meters long with a crew of twenty-two (twenty paddlers plus a drummer and sweeper/steersman). There's a smaller version, too, measuring 9 meters long with a crew of twelve.

Common racing formats are the 250-meter sprint and 2,000-meter endurance paddle. Races are typically held on rivers (the sport originated on China's Yangtze River), though modern competitions are also held on any enclosed, generally calm body of water.

★ **EQUIPMENT:**

Dragon boats are similar to canoes, which means they're also propelled by paddlers and not rowers (paddles are not connected to the boat, unlike attached rowing oars).

Traditional boats are made from hollowed-out teak trees, though there is no requirement to use teak—any wood is allowed, and modern boats are often made of fiberglass. Competi-tion boats are fully decorated with flags and dragon heads and tails, whereas practice boats are not.

★ **RULES AND TERMINOLOGY:**

The drummer is the boat's captain and guides paddlers with rhythmic drum beats to indicate when paddlers should begin and complete a synchronized stroke. Paddlers sit facing forward while the sweep sits at the back, also facing forward, to steer and guide the boat.

The International Dragon Boat Federation (IDBF; www.idbf.org) is the sport's international governing body and sponsors world championships every two years (the 2013 games will be hosted in Szeged, Hungary). Dragon boat races are also included in the Asian Games, the Southeast Asian Games, and the Asian Beach Games.

Less formal festival races—which typically encourage locals to enter and participate, regardless of previous experience—are held annually in dozens of major U.S. cities (New York, San Francisco, Portland, Boston, Washington DC) as well as internationally (Hong Kong, Sydney, Singapore, etc.).

ROWING

----- PROPEL A 62-FOOT-LONG BOAT WITH A SINGLE OAR, -----
FACING BACKWARDS

ROWING (COMMONLY CALLED "CREW" IN THE UNITED STATES) is one of the oldest Olympic sports. It was scheduled for the 1896 Olympics but canceled due to weather; it has been included in all since 1900. Crew is also a popular competitive sport in colleges and universities around the world. Rowing comes in many forms but all varieties share a core concept: rowers face backwards and use attached oars, in synchronized strokes, to propel their boats forward.

It's a simple concept, but don't underestimate the physical demands of modern rowing. The sport is highly technical, requiring precise coordination among rowers.

★ **BASIC CONCEPT:**

The modern sport uses sweep-oar boats (each rower holds a single oar with two hands) with a fixed number of crew (two, four, or eight) depending on the competitive category. Rowers each have a port or starboard position based on which side of the boat their oar is placed. In most cases a coxswain (steersman) shouts commands and steers the boat from either the bow (front) or stern (rear). In some events boats are coxless, in which case one of the rowing crew ties a cable to a foot in order to control the boat's rudder and direction in the water.

Most competitive rowing events, including the Olympics, run races in two categories: heavyweight/open and lightweight. Anybody can compete in the heavyweight/open category (rowing traditionally favors tall and muscular builds), whereas rowers in the lightweight category are restricted to a maximum of 160 pounds (men) and 130 pounds (women).

There are two main styles of racing: side-by-side and head races. In the former, boats line up side-by-side at a starting line and the race is won by the first boat to cross the finish line. The Olympics and the World Rowing Championships both feature side-by-side competitions covering 2,000 meters. Head races are time-based, with individual boats leaving at fixed intervals and competing for the best time over a set distance.

★ **EQUIPMENT:**

Rowing boats (called "shells") were originally made of wood but are now exclusively made of lightweight composite materials. Strict rules govern a boat's maximum length (between 34 and 62 feet, depending on crew size) and minimum weight (50 to 211 pounds). Rowers sit in sliding seats, attached to rollers, to maximize rowing efficiency. Surprisingly, there are no restrictions on the weight, size, or shape of the oar. That said, most competitive teams use oars 12 to 13 feet in length.

FAMOUS ROWING RACES

In terms of renown and prestige, three annual rowing races tower above all others: the Oxford-Cambridge and Harvard-Yale races (both covering 6.5 kilometers) and the Henley Royal Regatta (2,112 meters) held in Henley-on-Thames in Oxfordshire, England.

The Head of the River Race, held each March in London on the Thames River, is far and away the world's most prestigious head race, though the Head of the Charles Regatta held each October on Boston's Charles River is considered the world's largest head race.

Earning the title of the world's longest race is the two-day, 115-mile Corvallis to Portland Regatta (CPR — get it?) held each June in Oregon.

★ **WHERE TO PLAY AND WATCH:**

The summer Olympics are the best place to catch rowing at its most intense and competitive. The sport's governing body, the Fédération Internationale des Sociétés d'Aviron (FISA; www.worldrowing.com), organizes an annual World Rowing Championship as well as the annual World Rowing Cup. In the United States, U.S. Rowing (www.usrowing.org) organizes dozens of professional and amateur events across the country.

The main—and crucial—difference between sweep-oar rowing and sculling is the number of oars. Each rower controls a single oar in the former, two oars (one per hand) in the latter. Each sculler's right

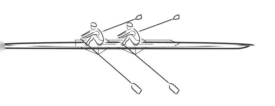

oar extends to the boat's port side, the left oar to starboard. Scull boats usually operate without a coxswain in teams of two, four, or eight (the Olympics features a solo sculling category, too).

Scullers have an added complication to deal with: overlapping oars. The sculler's oars meet in the middle twice during every stroke (once as the sculler lunges forward, and again as the sculler pulls the oars through the water). To prevent oars from colliding, scullers hold one hand above the other and/or slightly stagger the position of their oarlocks. Either way, the asymmetry puts extra stress on the sculler, burning precious additional energy.

YACHT RACING

----- WHEN IN DOUBT, LET IT OUT -----

THE WORLD OF COMPETITIVE SAILING is divided into two main categories: yachts and dinghies. Technically any recreational craft, as opposed to commercial and military boats, can properly be called a yacht. Yet these days racing yachts are always the larger seagoing vessels (as opposed to dinghies, which are smaller inshore harbor craft).

Boat racing is an ancient pursuit, with the earliest references dating to the third century BC. The modern sport of yacht racing dates to the nineteenth century and boats have raced in nearly every modern Olympics since 1900 (the sport was officially rebranded "sailing" starting at the 1996 Olympics, perhaps to shed the highfalutin connotations of the word "yacht").

Today there are recognized classes of racing yachts. Unlike most other global sports, there is no single international championship (excluding the Olympics) where the world's top boaters regularly compete. Instead there are dozens of prestigious long-standing competitions, held on nearly every major ocean, sea, river, and lake with favorable winds, where sailors compete and show off their boat-handling skills.

★ **BASIC CONCEPT:**

To control the boat efficiently and make the best use of the prevailing winds—at its heart sailing is a straightforward sport, and the goal of any yacht race is to be the fastest and most proficient boat on the

THE BIRTH OF COMPETITIVE SAILING

MOST SAILORS AGREE: the first modern yacht race was held in 1851 when the schooner America *won a race around the Isle of Wight in Britain. The trophy, renamed the America's Cup in the schooner's honor, was subsequently won by New York Yacht Club every single year until 1983—making it the longest winning streak in the history of any major sport. That year the America's Cup was won by the Royal Perth Yacht Club's* Australia II.

water. Of course, weather is unpredictable, and the elements play an important role in major races.

★ **EQUIPMENT**:

While there is no single standard for competitive yacht racing, there are common classes of yachts and dinghies. At the Olympics, for example, the following are some of the common boat classes that compete for medals:

> » *Laser: One-person single-sail dinghy, measuring 13 feet 10 inches long and weighing a minimum of 130 pounds.*

> » *Finn: One-person single-sail dinghy, measuring 14 feet 9 inches long and weighing a minimum of 320 pounds.*

> » *470: Two-person single-sail dinghy, measuring the eponymous 4.7 meters long (15.4 feet) with a minimum of 260 pounds.*

> » **49er:** *Two-person single-sail dinghy, measuring 16 feet long with a minimum of 163 pounds.*

> » **Star:** *Two-person, single-sail yacht, measuring 22 feet 8 inches long and weighing a minimum of 1,480 pounds.*

★ **WHERE TO PLAY AND WATCH:**

The summer Olympics are the best place to catch competitive sailing events. The America's Cup (www.americascup.com), the most famous non-Olympics yacht race, is held in various locations around the world whenever competing yacht clubs meet the race's requirements and earn the right to challenge the current cup holders (the next America's Cup takes place in San Francisco in 2013). Britain's esteemed Royal Ocean Racing Club (www.rorc.org) and Ireland's Royal Cork Yacht Club (www.royalcork.com) both sponsor popular races and regattas. In the United States, U.S. Sailing (www.ussailing.org) is the sport's national governing body and lists dozens of races and sailing events.

05

Bowling and Curling

CHAPTER FIVE

PÉTANQUE

----- GET CLOSE BUT DON'T TOUCH -----

ANY SPORT THAT INVOLVES TOSSING OR ROLLING A SMALL BALL is technically part of the "boules" family. The ancient Romans are credited with inventing the basic throw-a-ball-at-a-target concept (no doubt borrowing and improving from the ancient Greeks) and of introducing the game concept to the French.

Boules has always been incredibly popular in France and, in fact, the French are responsible for modernizing the ancient game of boules under the name *pétanque* in 1907. Today pétanque is popular across southern Europe and in any country where French immigrants have settled.

The first pétanque tournament was held in Provence, in southern France, in 1910. The first world championships were organized in 1959 by the sport's international governing body, the Fédération Internationale de Pétanque et Jeu Provençal (FIPJP; www.fipjp.com). The championships are held every two years and are contested by no fewer than forty-eight teams from countries as diverse as Pakistan, Niger, and Laos.

★ **BASIC CONCEPT:**

The aim of all boules games is for teams to throw large metal balls as close as possible to a jack (called the *cochonnet* in pétanque). At the end of each pétanque round only one team scores points, earning one point for every boule closer to the jack than their opponent's closest boule. Games of pétanque are typically played to 13 points.

★ **EQUIPMENT AND PLAYING SPACE:**

Boules must be made of metal and are roughly 3 inches in diameter and weigh 1.5 pounds. Balls are often engraved or marked with initials so players can identify their own boules. Jacks are small and round, with a diameter of about 1 inch. The playing field must be no smaller than 40 feet by 10 feet.

★ **RULES AND TERMINOLOGY:**

Pétanque is played three against three (triples), two against two (doubles), or one against one (singles). Each player starts with two boules (triples) or three boules (doubles and singles). Teams toss a coin to determine who gets to draw a circle on the ground, anywhere on the playing space, in which all players must stand and throw boules. The circle must be more than 1 meter (3 feet) from the nearest obstacle. A player from the leadoff team then throws the jack in any direction; it must land more than 6 meters (approximately 13 feet) from the circle and at least 1 meter from all obstacles or it is retossed. After throwing the jack, the same player throws the first boule.

PÉTANQUE

BOWLING & CURLING
★ C.05 ★

103

An opposing player then tries to place a boule closer to the jack or knock their opponent's boule away from the jack. The team farthest from the jack continues throwing until one of their boules is closest to the jack. When a team runs out of boules, the opposing team throws until they, too, run out.

Other important rules include:

> » *When throwing boules, the player's feet must stay flat on the ground and within the circle.*
>
> » *Boules must be thrown or rolled underarm.*
>
> » *Players on the same team do not have to alternate throws, but players must always toss their own boules.*
>
> » *Only one team can score points in each round.*
>
> » *If the jack is knocked out of bounds, no team scores (unless only one team has boules left, in which case they earn one point for each remaining boule).*

VARIANT » BOCCE

Bocce is the Italian version of pétanque (*bocce* is plural for the Italian word *boccia* or ball). The rules are similar, the main differences being the composition of the balls (bocce balls can be made of hard plastic) and the shape of the court (bocce courts are 60 to 90 feet long and 10 to 15 feet wide). The jack is called the *pallino* and teams most commonly field two players and four balls in total.

At the beginning of each round, two players from each team are positioned at opposite ends of the court. They must play the entire round from the end of the court where they started. Unlike in pétanque, bocce players do not start by drawing a shooting circle on the court; instead one team selects a side and throws the pallino at least 16 feet from their boundary line.

As in pétanque, the team with the ball closest to the pallino keeps tossing. A point is scored for the team with its ball closest to the pallino. Additional points are scored for each ball closer to the pallino than the closest ball of the opposing team.

The bocce toss is governed by strict rules. Players must throw the ball in one of three ways and announce which type in advance (and be acknowledged by the referee or opposing team):

Punto (point throw) is aimed at the pallino with the goal of leaving the ball as close as possible without hitting other balls along the way. Two points are scored if the ball touches the pallino (and stays that way for the entire game).

Raffa is aimed at another ball to knock it away.

Volo is an aerial throw aimed to knock either the pallino or another ball.

VARIANT » LAWN BOWLING

Lawn bowling is the most popular version of boules, or ball-rolling games, in the United Kingdom and Australia. The goals of lawn bowling and pétanque are similar—both involve rolling balls at a target, or jack, to earn points. What makes lawn bowling unique is the asymmetrical ball: in lawn bowling every ball has a subtle but noticeable bias that makes it roll in a curved line.

Lawn bowling is played on large grassy rectangles (usually immaculately groomed and precisely level). In all versions of the game, one team starts by placing a bowling mat at one end of the green and rolling the jack to the other end. Once the jack stops rolling, it is aligned to the center of its respective "rink" (bowling greens are divided into parallel playing strips known as rinks).

In lawn bowling each player starts with four balls (singles and doubles), three balls (triples), or two balls (fours). The gameplay and scoring are similar to pétanque in most other respects, with a major exception: in lawn bowling it is okay for a ball to stray out of bounds as long as it ends its roll within bounds.

Rounds of lawn bowling are called "ends" and are played to 21 or 25 points (called "shots" in lawn bowling) or to 21 or 25 ends of play (more common for triples and fours).

CURLING

----- LAWN BOWLING ON ICE -----

CURLING IS PART OF THE BOULES FAMILY OF GAMES. If you ignore the fact that curling is played on ice (instead of grass), there are plenty of similarities between curling and lawn bowling. In fact, both games share a northern European ancestry (the earliest references to curling date from sixteenth-century Scotland and Holland). Today the game is nearly synonymous with Canada. The Royal Montreal Curling Club is the oldest sporting club in North America (established in 1807) and generations of Canadians have grown up playing the game in school and university.

Curling was an Olympic demonstration sport as early as 1924; at the 1998 Olympics curling became part of the official games (Canada's men's team won silver, the women's team won gold). The

World Curling Federation (www.worldcurling.org) and USA Curling (www.curlingrocks.net) also host matches and championships throughout the year.

★ BASIC CONCEPT:

Two teams of four players take turns sliding heavy granite stones on an ice-covered surface known as a curling sheet. The goal is to slide the stones toward a circular target (called the "house") on the opposite end of the ice. Teams earn points for positioning their stones closest to the center (also known as the "button") of the circular target.

It's called an "end" once both teams have thrown all their stones. The team with the stone closest to the button wins the end and scores one point for each stone sitting closer to the button than the opponent's closest stone. Only the winning team scores points. Curling matches typically last for ten ends and the team with the higher overall score wins.

★ EQUIPMENT AND PLAYING SPACE:

The playing surface, called a curling sheet, measures 146 to 150 feet by 14½ to 16½ feet. The ice is covered with so-called "pebble," which refers to droplets of frozen water that cause curling stones to rotate slightly.

Curling stones are granite discs weighing 38 to 44 pounds with a maximum circumference of 36 inches. Handles are permanently attached to the top of the stones.

★ RULES AND TERMINOLOGY:

What sets curling apart from all other games is the sweepers (two per team). Sweepers are allowed to brush the ice in front of a moving curling stone in order to affect its trajectory (generally smoothing pebbles to speed up the stone, or to reduce spin). Other important rules:

» It's a penalty if any active player touches a moving stone with their body or broom. Players are expected to flag any violations and replace the stones as they would have ended up or remove the offending stone from play.

» Until four stones have been played (two per team), stones in the "free guard zone" (an area extending 21 feet from the button towards the center of the curling sheet) cannot be removed or knocked off by an opponent's stone. If they are removed, they are replaced in their original position and the offending stone is removed from play and cannot be used until the next end starts.

» In the case of a tie at the end of a match, play continues for as many ends as needed to break the tie.

» A game may be conceded if considered unwinnable. In ten-end matches, it's usually required for at least eight ends to be completed before a team is allowed to concede.

SHUFFLEBOARD

----- NOT JUST FOR THE OLD AND INFIRM -----

LET'S BE HONEST, SHUFFLEBOARD CONJURES IMAGES of old folks and somnolent cruise ships. This sport has a definite image problem. Shuffleboard is popular with the older crowd because it's competitive and yet requires minimal physical exertion. It's one sport that's yet to undergo a hipster "rediscovery" and subsequent trendy phase. Who knows, maybe the sport is due for a revival.

★ BASIC CONCEPT:

Use a paddle to slide a puck down a rectangular court, scoring points and knocking your opponent's pucks out of bounds. Players alternate sliding four pucks each (eight total per round) in the same direction and swapping directions at the end of each round. Games are typically won by the first player (or team) to score 50 or 100 points.

★ EQUIPMENT AND PLAYING SPACE:

While there's no global standard for shuffleboard courts, the general rule of thumb is a rectangle 35 to 40 feet long and 6 feet wide. The playing surface is always smooth (often coated with resin) and marked at either end with a scoring triangle (pointed towards center court). Each triangle is subdivided into four scoring sections: 10 points (top of the triangle), 8 points (next tier), 7 points (next tier), and -10 points (the nasty "10 Off" section at the bottom).

Pucks (called "biscuits" if you are of a certain age) are generally 6 inches in diameter and made of wood. Paddles have semicircular shoes at one end, used to push pucks down the court with accuracy.

★ RULES AND TERMINOLOGY:

Shuffleboard has precise scoring rules. Pucks must land completely inside a scoring area and not touch any lines in order to be scored. If the puck is even slightly touching the line, no points are earned. Points are calculated only once all eight pucks have been played. Any puck knocked out of bounds is immediately removed from the playing surface (and restored to the rightful player at the start of the next round).

TEN-PIN BOWLING

----- STRIKE! -----

BOWLING, AT LEAST THE TEN-PIN VARIETY, feels quintessentially American. Think of the bowling alley's hallowed place in 1950s and '60s American pop culture, or think of films like *The Big Lebowski*, *7-10 Split*, and *Kingpin*. Oddly enough the British are equally passionate (and quirky) about ten-pin bowling. Neither country can claim paternity of the game; bowling goes as far back as ancient Egypt and, in more modern times, derives from German nine-pin bowling and the ancient English game of skittles.

★ **BASIC CONCEPT:**

Ten-pin bowling is simple enough. Players take turns lofting large solid balls down a long rectangular alley, with the goal of knocking down as many pins as possible. The eponymous ten pins are typically controlled by a machine that sets and clears them automatically. At the start of each player's turn the pins are set into a triangle with pin 1 in the front row, pins 2 and 3 in the second row, pins 4 to 6 in the third row, and pins 7 to 10 in the back row.

Games of bowling last for ten frames, with each bowler rolling two balls per frame (up to three rolls in the tenth frame).

★ **EQUIPMENT AND PLAYING SPACE:**

Official bowling lanes measure 41½ inches wide and 60 feet from the foul line (where players must release their ball) to pin 1. Running alongside every lane is an out-of-bounds alley known as the gutter (no score for the roll). Balls have a maximum circumference of 27 inches and cannot weigh more than 16 pounds. Bowling pins must be 15 inches tall and weigh between 3 pounds 6 ounces and 3 pounds 10 ounces.

★ RULES AND TERMINOLOGY:

Newcomers can have a difficult time mastering the bowling scoring system, which tracks each player's score as well as their cumulative strikes and spares. The most basic score is when a player leaves one or more pins standing after two rolls—in this case, they earn the total number of pins knocked down.

When a player's first ball knocks down all ten pins it's called a strike (marked on the scorecard with an "X") and the player does not roll again until the next frame. A strike scores 10 points plus the points for the next two balls rolled. For example, player A rolls a strike in frame 3 and, in frame 4, knocks down five pins on the first throw and two pins on the second. That player scores 10 + 5 + 2 for a total of 17 points in frame 3 *and* 7 points in frame 4.

A spare (marked with a diagonal line) is when it takes two balls to knock down all ten pins. A spare scores 10 points plus the points earned for the next ball rolled (in the example above, if player A rolls a spare in frame 3 and, in frame 4, knocks down five pins on the first throw and two pins on the second, the player scores 10 + 5 for a total of 15 points in frame 3 *and* 7 points in frame 4).

When players roll consecutive strikes or spares, the point bonuses carry over. For example, player A rolls strikes in frames 3, 4, and 5 and scores 10 + 10 + 10 for a total of 30 points in frame 3 (the score for frames 4 and 5 won't be final until the player rolls more balls). This means 30 is the maximum score per frame, and 300 is the maximum score per game (one strike each in frames 1 through 9 plus three strikes in the tenth frame).

Players who roll a strike in the tenth frame earn two extra rolls to calculate bonus points (these extra points don't count on their own, they only count for calculating the initial strike's score). Similarly, if you roll a spare in the tenth frame you earn one extra roll to calculate bonus points.

★ **WHERE TO PLAY AND WATCH**:

Thousands of bowling alleys are located throughout North America and western Europe. Ten-pin bowling surely must be one of the world's most accessible mainstream sports. Bowling is also popular on television, with dozens of professional tournaments organized each year by governing bodies such as the United States Bowling Congress (USBC; www.bowl.com), the Professional Bowlers Association (PBA; www.pba.com), and the British Tenpin Bowling Association (BTBA; www.btba.org.uk).

VARIANT » NINE-PIN BOWLING

This mainly European sport (and, oddly enough, also popular in Texas) uses smaller balls and smaller lanes. Pins are set in a diamond shape, with the center pin typically painted red (in non-tournament play, the red pin earns extra points when it remains standing and all other pins are knocked down).

Players roll twice per turn even if they knock down all pins on the first roll. In competitive play teams have up to six players each, with each player throwing up to 120 times per game (30 deliveries per player rotating across four separate lanes). The team knocking over the most pins wins.

VARIANT » FIVE-PIN BOWLING

This Canadian version of the sport uses even smaller balls (the size of your hand) and even smaller pins (about three-quarter size compared to ten-pin). The pins are arranged in a "V" with the center pin worth 5 points when knocked over, the next two pins worth 3 points each, and the outermost pins worth 2 points each (for a total score of 15 points).

VARIANT » CANDLEPIN BOWLING

New Englanders take candlepin bowling very seriously, no doubt because the sport was invented in Worcester, Massachusetts, in the 1880s. Candlepin bowling is identical to ten-pin bowling with three critical exceptions. First, candlepin balls are puny, measuring 4½ inches in diameter and weighing no more than 2½ pounds. Second, the pins are small, cylindrical, and lightweight (looking something like a candle). Finally, any knocked-down pins (known as "dead wood") are not removed from the lane but instead become potential obstacles.

U.B.S.

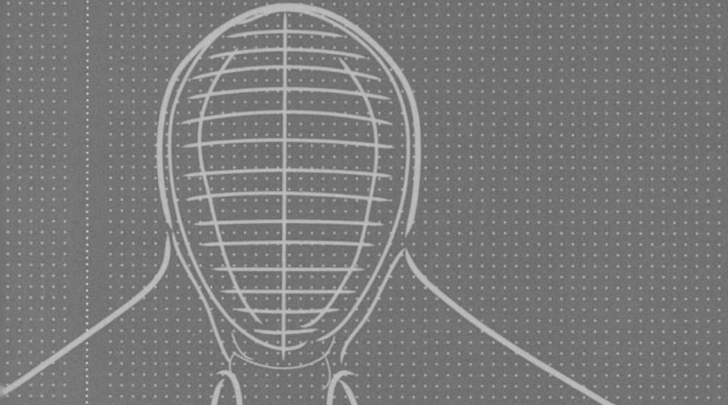

★ ⋯⋯ **06** ⋯⋯ ★

Combat Sports
CHAPTER SIX

MARTIAL ARTS

THERE ARE DOZENS OF MARTIAL ARTS SYSTEMS, but the most famous ones all share a common ancestry in Asia. The name itself honors the Roman god of war, Mars, and all martial arts promote direct person-to-person combat at some level. Yet it's not true that all martial arts are violent. The majority, in fact, combine philosophical concepts such as self-discovery and spiritual development with physical fitness and self-defense (as opposed to offense).

★ **AIKIDO: BASIC CONCEPT**

Aikido evolved from traditional jujitsu in the 1920s. Its founder, Morihei Ueshiba, had a unique vision for the sport: to foment peace and reconciliation. Aikido requires less physical strength than other martial arts. The emphasis is on mirroring an attacker's movements and momentum, and redirecting them (as opposed to resisting them). The name *aikido* means "the way of harmonious spirit." It has practitioners around the world and is the basis for a lifelong pursuit of physical and mental acuity.

Aikido training typically features two partners engaging in set movements. An attacker (the *uke*) initiates a movement, which is then neutralized by the opposing partner (the *nage*). There are dozens of attack and defensive techniques in aikido, as well as weapon training with staffs, swords, and knives.

★ **CAPOEIRA: BASIC CONCEPT**

Part dance and part martial art, capoeira is Brazil's contribution to the world of combat sports. Capoeira started as a way for African slaves in Brazil to practice self-defense in the form of dance (slaves could not openly practice martial arts). Fighting moves include kicking, leg sweeps, head butts, and elbow jabs. These movements have always been set to music, and nowadays capoeira resembles a tightly choreographed dance mixing acrobatics with dodging, fighting, and sparring.

Capoeira bouts are rowdy, noisy affairs with musicians playing a beat that defines the match rhythm. Two capoeiristas enter a circle and face off, using combinations of fluid attacking and defensive moves. Often there are no strikes at all, since part of the sport's philosophy is to fake out opponents and avoid attacks using evasive moves. The bout ends when one capoeirista concedes by sitting down when other capoeiristas replace one or both players, or when a musician determines it.

★ JUDO: BASIC CONCEPT

The founder of modern judo, Jigoro Kano, was a nineteenth-century master of jujitsu. At the time the ancient practice of jujitsu was unpopular in an increasingly westernized Japan, and Kano had a hard time attracting students to study with him. Kano was a marketing genius: he rebranded his version of jujitsu as "judo" and added a spiritual element to the practice (the concept of *do* in judo means the "path" or "way"). Kano's judo became a philosophy for living all aspects of one's life.

Judo focuses on three groups of techniques: throwing, grappling, and striking. In competition, judo matches typically have a standing phase (opponents attempt to throw each other) and a ground phase (once an opponent is on the ground, then both opponents can use a hold down, literally holding an opponent down for 15 to 25 seconds, or using a choke hold or similar controlling technique to force an opponent to submit).

Judo became an official Olympic sport at the 1964 games in Tokyo (in 1992 for women). Judo at the Olympics is divided into weight classes and scored based on a tiered point system for throwing the opponent to the ground, pinning an opponent to the ground on their back, or forcing an opponent to submit using a choke hold or arm lock.

★ JUJITSU: BASIC CONCEPT

Jujitsu is the mother of all Japanese martial arts and one of its oldest forms. Its lineage can be traced to the fourteenth century when it was used to train samurai warriors how to defeat an armed opponent without using a weapon, the theory being that armored samurai were generally impervious to sword attacks. As a result, jujitsu training places emphasis on throwing, pinning, choke holds, joint locks, and similar controlling techniques. Underlying all jujitsu teaching is learning how to use your opponents' own force against them (as opposed to resisting or opposing their force directly).

6 BEST
MARTIAL ARTS MOVIES, EVER

★ **FISTS OF FURY** (1971).
The first, and arguably best, Bruce Lee film and
the film responsible for the 1970s martial arts fad.

★ **THE KARATE KID** (1984).
Miyagi catching a fly with chopsticks? Priceless.

★ **FIST OF LEGEND** (1994).
Jet Li's finest work.

★ **SEVEN SAMURAI** (1954).
The classic film by Akira Kurosawa.

★ **THE WAY OF THE DRAGON** (1972).
The Bruce Lee fights Chuck Norris in the final scene—
how cool is that!

★ **THE LEGEND OF DRUNKEN MASTER** (1994).
Jackie Chan in one of the best—and weirdest—
movies in the genre.

Numerous branches of Japanese martial arts—including aikido and judo—have evolved from the ancient practice of jujitsu. Modern jujitsu was never as famous or popular as judo or karate until 1993 and the launch of the Ultimate Fighting Championships. This was a made-in-television-heaven concept: a pay-per-view competition devoted to determining the most effective martial art style for unarmed combat situations. Fighters entered an octagonal cage and fought with minimal rules until a fighter was knocked out, submitted in defeat, or was too injured to compete. One of the early fighters, Royce Gracie, used little-known techniques from the related Brazilian Jin-Jitsu to defeat much larger opponents, giving jujitsu a major promotional boost.

★ **KARATE: BASIC CONCEPT**

While karate is based on an ancient martial art developed on what is today the Japanese island of Okinawa, the sport's modern form is a product of the twentieth century. In 1922 a karate teacher from Okinawa, Gichin Funakoshi, gave a demonstration in Tokyo; by the late 1930s Funakoshi's version of karate (called Shotokan karate) was ubiquitous in schools and universities across Japan. The self-discipline inherent in Shotokan karate, as well as its aggressive attacking styles, were a good fit for a militaristic Japan bent on regional expansion (at the time Japan was fighting a war with China and on the cusp of attacking the United States at Pearl Harbor).

The practice of karate is both a physical and spiritual pursuit. Karate stresses self-awareness and the development of personal qualities such as fearlessness, honor, and virtue. As a martial art, karate emphasizes striking postures: kicking, punching, open-hand blows, and, in some variants, the use of weapons. Karate's distinctive white robes and colored-belt grading system date from the 1920s and were inspired by the founder of judo. Each belt has different degrees, called *kyu*, usually numbered from 10 (novice) to 1 (master). Color rankings vary by school and there is no global standard, though generally the progression is from white (novice) to yellow, orange, green, blue, purple, brown, and black (master).

★ KENDO: BASIC CONCEPT

Kendo is the art of fencing samurai-style. Along with archery and horseback riding, sword fighting was one of the disciplines required of samurai warriors. The name means "way of the sword" in Jap-

anese and combatants face off with bamboo swords and stamp their feet and shout as they strike and thrust at each other.

Like most Japanese martial arts, kendo has a strong spiritual aspect, in this case Buddhism. It's impossible to become a kendo master without embarking on a quest for spiritual

enlightenment. It's also impossible to become a master without some serious protective gear! Modern kendo armor consists of four pieces: helmet (*men*), body protector (*do*), gloves (*kote*), and hip and groin protector (*tare*).

★ NGUNI STICK FIGHTING: BASIC CONCEPT

Stick fighting is a fairly common ritual in Africa. In South Africa members of the Nguni tribe are famous for battling with two large sticks, one for offense and one for defense. Sometimes a shield is allowed; otherwise no armor or protection is used. Combatants simply face off with their sticks and fight until dominance is established by one fighter. It's a brutal and violent spectacle. The two fighters don't hold back, stopping only to replace any sticks that break.

★ TAE KWON DO: BASIC CONCEPT

Korea's national sport tae kwon do, which can be translated literally as "the way of kicking and punching," is all about high, fast-moving kicks. The origins of the sport are ancient, with references in Korean history dating back thousands of years. Tae kwon do started as a defensive practice, a way of conditioning the body and mind. Over the years it has been influenced by martial arts styles from across China and Japan. It's also a sport with a strong moral code and spiritual philosophy that can be boiled down to a pursuit of harmony between mind, body, and society at large.

Today, along with judo, tae kwon do is a full-fledged Olympic sport with millions of practitioners. In competitive settings, matches last three rounds and points are scored for accurate, legal, and powerful strikes to an opponent (light strikes do not score points). One point is scored for a kick or punch to the torso, 2 points are scored for a spinning kick and 3 points are scored for a kick to the head. At the end of a match the competitor with the most points wins (ties are decided in a sudden-death fourth round). A competitor loses the match if they are knocked out by a legal strike.

BOXING

----- WHEN THE BELL RINGS, COME OUT FIGHTING -----

BOXING IS AN ANCIENT ART. It's likely that men have met in bare-knuckled battled since the dawn of time. The first direct evidence of boxing as it is known today comes from ancient Greece: boxing was part of the original Olympic games and was governed by strict rules of engagement (including the use of gloves).

England is where the modern sport evolved. Starting in the sixteenth century, innovations and improvements to boxing were made through rules published before major public fights or boxing tournaments. Rules were eventually codified and covered the length of rounds, ring size, definition of weight classes, what parts of the body were off-limits, and other restrictions fully recognizable today. The so-called Marquess of Queensberry rules, published in 1867 and named after their British patron, remain the guiding principles of the modern sport.

These days boxers are divided into two categories: pro and amateur. The concept of "amateur" came of age with the modern Olympics in the late nineteenth century. Amateurs are not allowed to fight for money, and their bouts are limited to three or four rounds with scoring based on technical merit (as opposed to physical impact). Pro boxers, on the other hand, compete for money, and spectators typically bet on the results of the match.

★ ★ ★ ★ ★ ·········· U.B.S. ·········· ★ ★ ★ ★ ★

BOXING

Boxing is a popular Olympic sport (men have contended for medals since the 1904 games). Women boxers competed for the first time ever at the 2012 Olympics in London.

★ **BASIC CONCEPT:**

Two competitors (sometimes called fighters or pugilists) hit each other with glove-encased fists while avoiding each other's blows. Fights (sometimes called bouts) are divided into a preset number of rounds, typically 3 minutes long, with short rest intervals between rounds. A ringing bell traditionally sounds the start and end of each round. Amateur fights last three to four rounds and pro fights last four to twelve rounds. All officially sanctioned championship fights last twelve rounds.

Fights are supervised by a single referee and generally scored by a panel of judges (sometimes the referee is also a judge). There are four outcomes in a fight: a fighter is knocked out and unable to get up before the referee counts to ten seconds (called a knockout or KO); the referee determines a fighter is too injured to continue (called a technical knockout or TKO); a fighter is disqualified for breaking a rule; or, if none of the above happens by the end of the last round, a winner is declared by the referee or judges, based on points scored during the bout.

Fights are organized by weight classes. Originally there were eight professional classes: flyweight (up to 112 pounds), bantamweight (118 pounds), featherweight (126 pounds), lightweight (135 pounds), welterweight (147 pounds), middleweight (160 pounds), light heavyweight (175 pounds), and heavyweight (no restrictions).

★ **EQUIPMENT AND PLAYING SPACE:**

The traditional boxing ring is actually a square, measuring 16 to 20 feet per side and enclosed by ropes to prevent fighters from falling out. Boxing gloves have been required since 1892 and must weigh no less than 8 ounces each in sanctioned pro fights.

Almost universally, boxers are not allowed to hit below their opponent's belt; hit their opponent's neck, back, kidneys, or back of the head; or bite, scratch, gouge, trip, push, grab, or hold their opponent. Here are other important boxing rules:

> » *Boxers cannot hit with an open glove, the inside of the glove, wrist, backhand, or side of the hand.*

> » *If boxers are knocked out of the ring, they get a count of 20 seconds to get back in and cannot be assisted.*

> » *When a boxer is knocked down, the opposing fighter must immediately move to the farthest neutral corner.*

> » *In amateur boxing, when a boxer looks to be in physical jeopardy, the referee may call a "standing eight count" and separate the boxers for a count of 8 seconds to allow for recovery. In some jurisdictions a "three knockdown rule" means a technical knockdown is awarded when a fighter is knocked down three times in a match.*

> » *Despite rumors to the contrary, a boxer who is knocked down cannot be "saved by the bell" in any round (though this varies by jurisdiction).*

★ **WHERE TO PLAY AND WATCH:**

Boxing is popular in neighborhood gyms and sports clubs, though mainly as a form of exercise. If you want to try competitive boxing, you'll need to track down a local boxing club.

Boxing has four competing governing bodies, each of which hosts its own title matches in the major weight classes: World Boxing Association (WBA), World Boxing Organization (WBO), International Boxing Federation (IBF), and World Boxing Council (WBC).

VARIANT » KICKBOXING

Kickboxing is essentially boxing with hands and feet. It's the ultimate stand-up combat sport, developed in Japan in the 1960s and borrowing heavily from Thai and Western boxing as well as judo and karate. The sport is unapologetically hybrid, in that it constantly borrows effective techniques from any martial arts discipline.

Opponents are generally allowed to strike each other with fists and feet above the hip (lower body strikes are allowed in Japanese and international competitions, though the crotch is always off-limits). In American and international competitions opponents cannot strike with knees or elbows (in Japanese competitions knee thrusts are allowed). Matches are usually three to ten rounds lasting 2 to 3 minutes each.

VARIANT » MUAY THAI

Muay Thai is the Thai version of kickboxing and the national sport of Thailand. What makes it different from Japanese and American kickboxing is that knee and elbow strikes are allowed—Muay Thai is known as the "art of eight limbs" because it allows contact by feet, hands, elbows, and knees. Another key difference is that Muay Thai opponents are allowed to clinch each other (in fact, knee and elbow strikes are most effective in a clinch). No surprise, Muay Thai requires intensive body conditioning. The sport is not easy on its practitioners.

5 BEST BOXING MATCHES, EVER

★ **JOE LOUIS VS. MAX SCHMELING** (1938).
The American Joe Louis had lost to the German
Max Schmeling in 1936. Two years later, with Adolf
Hitler leading Germany into World War II, Louis and
Schmeling had a rematch. Louis managed a first-
round knockout and Schmeling went home a very
disappointed Nazi.

★ **SONNY LISTON VS. CASSIUS CLAY** (1964).
Sonny Liston was an overwhelming favorite to beat
Cassius Clay (aka Muhammad Ali) when they met
for their first fight in Miami. Liston conceded the
match in the sixth round, claiming a hurt shoulder.
This is the fight where Clay earned the nickname
"The Greatest" and pranced around the ring shouting,
"I'm the greatest!"

- ★ **GEORGE FOREMAN VS. MUHAMMAD ALI** (1974).
  This is the famous "Rumble in the Jungle" of Zaire,
  when the aging Muhammad Ali fought to regain his
  title against heavyweight champion George Foreman.
  Ali won it in the eighth round, with the fight announcer
  famously saying of Ali, "Oh my God! He's won the
  title back at thirty-two!"

- ★ **MARVELOUS MARVIN HAGLER VS.
  SUGAR RAY LEONARD** (1987).
  The confluence of a massive television audience
  and sold-out Las Vegas crowd (the fight was hosted
  at Caesars Palace hotel) made this boxing's most
  famous fight of the decade. The fact that Hagler
  quit boxing after losing this match, following a controversial decision based on points in Leonard's
  favor, only adds to the legend.

- ★ **MIKE TYSON VS. EVANDER HOLYFIELD** (1997).
  Yeah, it's the heavyweight title fight where Tyson bit
  off a section of Holyfield's ear. Enough said, really.

FENCING

----- PARRY, RIPOSTE -----

THE ART OF FENCING—a word that simply means fighting with swords—is ancient. These days fencing is an umbrella term for three styles of blade-to-blade combat: foil, sabre, and épée. All three styles have been contested at the Olympics since the first modern games in 1896.

★ **BASIC CONCEPT:**

Foil features a slim rounded blade that scores only when the tip legally touches an opponent's torso or back (but not the arms). Sabre features an edged blade that scores for any strike touching an opponent from the waist up (excluding the hands) with either the point or edge. Épée uses a heavier blade and targets the entire body, though only strikes with the tip earn points.

The three styles have very different pacing. In foil, matches are paused each time a competitor's strike lands off-target. This is not the case in sabre or épée—the fighting continues nonstop.

In foil and sabre only a single strike can score at one time, and both styles use the concept of "right of way" to determine which fencer had the legal right to attack or riposte (i.e., counterattack) and thus score. The idea is that the fencer who commences the attack earns the right to score, unless the attack misses the opponent or is parried (i.e., deflected by the opponent's weapon).

U.B.S.

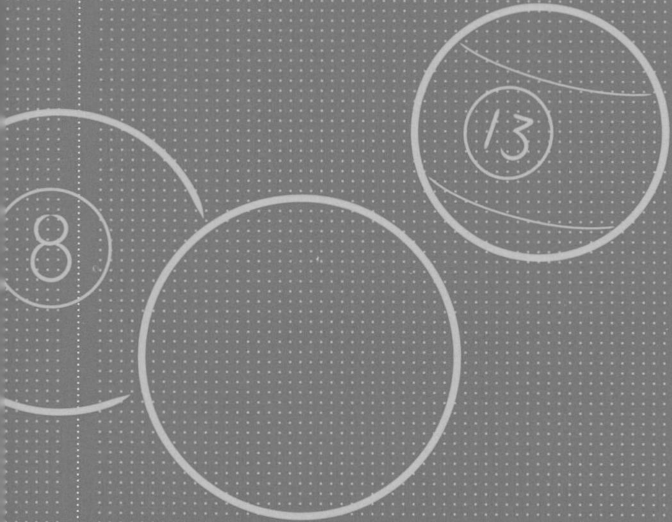

>>

Cue Sports

CHAPTER SEVEN

>>

ULTIMATE
Book of Sports

CUSHION BILLIARDS

----- POOL WITHOUT POCKETS -----

ALONG WITH POOL AND SNOOKER, CUSHION BILLIARDS (sometimes called carom billiards) is one of the main varieties of cue sports. What makes cushion billiards stand out from the other games? The lack of pockets. All cushion games are played on pocketless tables, with the general idea being to score points by knocking a cue ball into one or two other balls on a single shot.

★ **BASIC CONCEPT:**

Three-cushion carom, the most popular version of cushion billiards, is played by two competing players for points. Players take turns striking their cue ball towards the object balls; in order to score, the cue ball must touch a cushion at least three times (if the ball has spin on it and touches the same cushion twice, it does count as two touches) before striking the second object ball.

★ **EQUIPMENT AND PLAYING SPACE:**

Cues in cushion games are generally shorter and lighter than standard pool-hall cues. The striking tip is also narrower. Balls are about 20 percent heavier than standard pool balls and come in sets of three: one red "object" ball and two white cue balls (one with a small black dot to help tell it apart). In international games, three-cushion carom tables are always heated to roughly 10° Fahrenheit above room temperature, which makes the balls roll faster across the felt.

★ **RULES AND TERMINOLOGY:**

Players lag to determine who breaks. When breaking, it's a foul if the player does not strike the red ball before any other ball. On all subsequent shots either the red ball or the opponent's cue ball can be used as the first object ball. Points can be scored in numerous ways:

» *The cue ball strikes the first object ball and then strikes three (or more) cushions before striking the second object ball.*

» *The cue ball strikes three or more cushions and then strikes the two object balls.*

» *The cue ball strikes three or more cushions, then strikes the first object ball, then strikes one or more cushions, and then strikes the second object ball.*

» *The cue ball strikes two cushions, then strikes the first object ball, and then strikes one or more cushions before striking the second object ball.*

POOL

----- THE CLASSIC BILLIARDS GAME -----

POOL (CALLED "POCKET BILLIARDS" BY TRADITIONALISTS) is a broad family of games encompassing such familiar names as eight-ball, straight pool, and nine-ball. The object of all pool games is to sink specified balls into pockets, and without exception all games in this category require tables with pockets (six is the standard number).

Pool is a highly competitive sport, particularly at the national and international levels (pool is played professionally in more than fifty countries, from Korea to the Philippines to Russia). All sanctioned tournaments are governed by the World Pool-Billiard Association (WPA; www.wpa-pool.com), while the World Confederation of Billiard Sports (WCBS; www.billiard-wcbs.org) is the organization fighting for all three major cue categories (cushion, pool, and snooker) to be included in the Olympics (though, sadly, the 2020 games are the earliest likely games where cue sports will be played).

★ **BASIC CONCEPT**:

In eight-ball, the world's most popular and broadly played pool game, the object is to sink the eight ball. Each rack contains fifteen colored balls, with balls 1 to 7 called "solids" and balls 9 to 15 called "stripes" based on the balls' color and design. Players are assigned solids or stripes based on the first ball legally sunk, and must then sink all their assigned balls before legally pocketing the eight ball.

★ **EQUIPMENT:**

Standard pool tables are typically 4 feet by 8 feet or 4½ feet by 9 feet, with the general rule being that a table's length must be twice the length of its width measured cushion to opposite cushion.

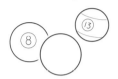

Balls must weigh between 5½ and 6 ounces and have a diameter of 2¼ inches. Official pool cues have a minimum length of 40 inches (no maximum) and can weigh no more than 25 ounces.

★ **RULES AND TERMINOLOGY:**

Here are some of the most important rules in the international version of eight-ball pool.

> » **Racking:** *Balls are racked in a triangle with the eight ball in the center of the triangle, the first ball of the rack on the circular spot marked on the felt, and a stripe and solid ball in alternating corners of the rack.*

> » **Breaking:** *A break is considered valid only when at least one ball is pocketed or at least four numbered balls touch a cushion. Otherwise the break is a foul and the opposing player can accept the table position as is or rerack the balls and choose themselves or their opponent to rebreak. If the eight ball is pocketed on the break, the breaker can rerack the balls or spot the eight ball and continue playing. The choice of stripes or solids is never determined on the break; it is only determined when a player legally pockets a ball* after *the break shot. If a stripe or solid ball is pocketed on the break, the ball(s) remains pocketed but the breaker is* not *assigned stripes or solids.*

> » **Open Table:** *The first player to legally sink a solid or stripe is assigned that group for the duration of the game. The table is "open" when neither player has legally sunk a stripe or solid*

ball. At this point it is legal to first strike any ball (solid or stripe) in order to sink any stripe or solid ball. If a player first strikes the eight ball, it's considered a foul and the shooter is not assigned solid or stripes; instead the shooter loses their turn and the table remains open. On an open table, all illegally pocketed balls remain pocketed.

» **Shooting:** Players must always call their shots (i.e., indicate what ball will be pocketed in which pocket) in advance unless the ball and pocket targets are obvious. Opponents are always allowed to inquire which ball and/or pocket is being targeted. Bank and combination shots are never obvious and should always be called. Except on breaks and when the table is open, shooters must first strike one of their own solid or stripe balls and *pocket a ball or force any numbered ball to touch a cushion.* Combination shots are allowed (i.e., it is legal to strike a solid into a solid ball, or a stripe into a stripe, in order to pocket the latter ball as long as the shot is called in advance). The eight ball can never be struck first in a combination shot, though it can be included in a multi-ball combination shot.

» **Fouls:** Balls pocketed on a foul remain pocketed, no exceptions! When a shooter fouls, the opponent is said to get "ball in hand" and is allowed to place the cue ball anywhere on the table and shoot the cue ball in any direction. It's a foul if any numbered ball is jumped or shot off the table. It's also a foul if a shooter does not have at least one foot in contact with the floor at the point of impact with the cue ball. The game is immediately lost if a shooter fouls when pocketing the eight ball (except on the break); inadvertently pockets the eight ball on the same shot used to sink the last of their assigned stripe or solid balls; jumps the eight ball off the table at any time; or sinks the eight ball out of turn.

5 FAMOUS POOL HALL QUOTES

★ "Do you like to gamble, Eddie? Gamble money on pool games?"
—*JACKIE GLEASON TO PAUL NEWMAN IN* THE HUSTLER *(1961)*

★ "You couldn't find big time if you had a road map."
—*PAUL NEWMAN TO TOM CRUISE IN* THE COLOR OF MONEY *(1986)*

★ "Beating a man out of his money, that's easy. Anybody can do that. But beating a man out of his money and making him like it…that's an art."
—*CHAZZ PALMINTERI IN* POOLHALL JUNKIES *(2002)*

★ "I'm just a pool player. There's probably no less important thing on the face of the earth. But mark this in your book: I'm the best. It's a proud thing to be the best at anything. But you wouldn't know anything about that."
—*FATS BROWN, PLAYED BY JONATHAN WINTERS IN "A GAME OF POOL" EPISODE OF* THE TWILIGHT ZONE *(1961)*

★ "Gee, practice really does make perfect!"
—*BOBBY BRADY, IN "THE HUSTLER" EPISODE OF* THE BRADY BUNCH (1974)

» **Winning:** *The game is won by the shooter who first pockets their group of balls, and then legally pockets the eight ball. The eight ball must be pocketed solely and directly, never in combination with any other ball(s).*

★ **WHERE TO PLAY AND WATCH:**

You can watch professional-level play at the annual World Nine-Ball Championship and World Eight-Ball Championship, and at dozens of amateur and professional tournaments held around the world. In the United States, the Billiard Congress of America (BCA; www.bca-pool.com) sanctions numerous events for all levels of players.

VARIANT » STRAIGHT POOL

Ask your grandparents about pool, and they'll likely talk about straight pool. This is the traditional version of the sport, immortalized in such films as *The Hustler*. The main difference between straight pool and games like eight-ball and nine-ball is that straight shooters can legally sink any ball on the table, in any combination.

The object of the game is to score points, with one point awarded for each legally pocketed ball (professional matches are played to 150 points). It doesn't matter how the ball reaches the pocket; a point is awarded as long as the called ball falls into the called pocket. Most fouls result in a one-point deduction from the shooter's score. The traditional rack puts the one ball and five ball in the far corners, away from the breaker, with all other balls placed randomly.

VARIANT » NINE-BALL

Nine-ball is a faster-paced alternative to straight pool and eight-ball. The quick pace lends itself to television broadcasting, which helps to explain why nine-ball is the fastest-growing sport within the billiards family.

Nine-ball is played on any standard pool table, but only nine balls (numbered 1 to 9) plus the cue are used. The object of the game is to sink the nine ball. One twist is that on every shot the cue ball must first touch the lowest-numbered ball on the table before touching any other ball. A second twist is that any ball can be pocketed at any time, so long as the lowest-numbered ball is touched first. As a result, most nine-ball games revolve around combination and bank shots that target the lowest-numbered ball on first touch, then the nine ball on second touch or ensuing combination touches.

The bottom line: nine-ball is not a "call your pocket" game, so as long as the lowest-numbered ball is first touched by the cue ball, it doesn't matter how the nine ball is subsequently pocketed on the same stroke. The nine ball can be pocketed for a win at any time, even on the break.

VARIANT » BUMPER POOL

Bumper pool is a simple—and addictive—billiards game. It's played on an octagonal or rectangular table about half the size of a traditional pool table. Two pockets are centered on the cushions at opposite ends of the table, separated by twelve to fourteen bumpers (fixed obstacles) spread across the table in the shape of a cross. Two bumpers also protect each pocket.

Players each start with five balls colored white or red (there is no cue ball, though one ball is marked in each set). The goal is to sink all five balls into the competitor's pocket at the far end of the table. Players start by lining up their five balls on the table at premarked positions, then strike their marked ball simultaneously at the far pocket, banking off the cushion to their right. If both players make the shot, they repeat the simultaneous shot. If one or both players miss the first shot, the player who sank a ball or came closest to the pocket shoots next. Since there is no cue ball, players simply strike the balls directly. A player's marked ball must be sunk before the player can sink their other balls. The first player to sink all five balls wins.

SNOOKER

----- POOL PLAYED ON A LARGE TABLE WITH SMALL BALLS AND -----
EVEN SMALLER POCKETS

SNOOKER IS TECHNICALLY A VERSION OF POOL. However, since the game is played on a unique table—with distinct balls, equipment, and scoring rules—snooker is given its own category in international tournaments and world championships.

The game is distinctly British (though increasingly popular in China), and is said to have been invented by nineteenth-century British servicemen stationed in India. Snooker was one of the first sporting events televised in color on British television. By the late 1970s snooker was all the rage in Britain and British Commonwealth countries.

★ BASIC CONCEPT:

The object of snooker is to score points by pocketing (called "potting" in snooker) balls in a predefined order. Snooker games start with a rack of fifteen red-colored balls that are each valued at 1 point. Games also start with six colored balls: yellow (2 points), green (3 points), brown (4 points), blue (5 points), pink (6 points), and black (7 points).

On every stroke players must first pot a red ball in order to legally pot a non-red ball on the shooter's ensuing stroke. If a non-red ball is potted, after the stroke it is returned to its original position on the table and can be repotted immediately on the next stroke. Once all red balls are potted, players pot the remaining balls in numerical order (yellow through black without returning them to the table). When the last ball is potted, the highest score wins.

In snooker, games are called "frames" and matches are usually played best-of-five or best-of-seven frames (professional matches are often best-of-seventeen or nineteen frames, and up to thirty-five frames at the world championships).

★ EQUIPMENT AND PLAYING SPACE:

Standard snooker tables are 6 feet wide and 12 feet long. All tables have a "baulk line" drawn across the width 29 inches above and parallel to the table's bottom cushion. A half-circle with a radius of 11½ inches is drawn from the center of the baulk line; when a player is "in hand" the cue ball is placed inside the half-circle. Snooker pockets are no more than 3½ inches across (about 20 percent smaller than standard pool pockets) and have rounded edges instead of angled corners (which require more accurate shots than in standard pool).

Here are some basic rules governing international snooker.

> » **Racking:** *The non-red balls start the game in a specific order (all tables have spots marking official placements): green-brown-yellow on the baulk line, blue in the middle of the table, and, at the opposite end, pink immediately in front and black several inches behind the red ball rack.*

> » **Breaking:** *The breaker starts with cue ball in hand within the half-circle and must cause the cue ball to touch a red ball. There is no other breaking requirement. If a red ball is not touched, or if the cue ball fouls in any other way, the opposing player can accept the table as is and continue play, or force the breaker to rerack and rebreak.*

> » **Shooting:** *With any red balls on the table, a shooter must first pot a red ball before any non-red ball. There's no requirement to call red balls, and any legally potted red balls are scored. After a red ball is potted, the shooter scores one point and can attempt to pot (but is not forced to pot—the shooter can target a red ball) a non-red ball on the next stroke. Shots on non-red balls must be called out in advance. If the shooter successfully pots a non-red ball, the value of the potted ball is scored, the potted ball is returned to its original location on the table, and the shooter earns an additional stroke to pot a red ball. If no red balls remain on the table, the shooter attempts to pot the remaining balls in order of value from yellow to black.*

> » **Fouls:** *Red balls that are illegally potted or fouled remain off the table, while all other balls are returned to their original table positions when illegally potted. The minimum penalty for a foul is 4 points; if a player fouls on the blue, pink, or black*

balls, the foul is scored at 5, 6, or 7 points respectively. When shooting for red, the cue ball must first touch a red ball (any other outcome is a foul). Players cannot jump balls, and any ball that falls off the table is considered foul. When the cue ball is touching another ball, the referee calls out "touching ball" and the shooter simply plays away from the touching ball without incurring a foul (since first contact is deemed to have been made with the touching ball).

» **Snookered:** The cue ball is said to be "snookered" when there is no visible, straight line to target the appropriate next ball. Snookering is a crucial part of every game, and is used to force an opponent into near-impossible starting positions (and thereby score points from the likely foul).

08

Cycling
CHAPTER EIGHT

BMX

----- BIG AIR ON A BIKE -----

BMX (BICYCLE MOTOCROSS) BEGAN as a stripped-down version of motocross (the motorized version) by former motorcycle racers and enthusiastic teenagers on vacant dirt lots in Southern California in the early 1970s. By 2008 BMX was a full-medal sport at the Olympics. Very few sports go from total nonexistence to official inclusion in the Olympics in less than four decades. BMX is one of the rare few to enjoy such phenomenal growth.

Early sanctioning bodies with colorful acronyms such as B.U.M.S. (Bicycle United Motocross Society) played a critical role marketing the BMX concept. By 1982, when BMX hosted its first international championships in Ohio, it was the fastest-growing sport in the United States. BMX has been a consistently featured sport at the alternative X Games competitions held annually in the United States.

Modern BMX is considered a "safe" contact sport (riders are required to wear safety gear, including helmets) and statistically BMX causes fewer injuries per participant than either football or basketball. BMX is also considered a family sport (no doubt because many of its top riders are teenagers).

★ **BASIC CONCEPT:**

BMX races generally pit four to eight riders racing against each other, the winner being the first to cross the finish line. BMX tracks often

feature challenging terrain including jumps and obstacles. Racers compete in different categories based on wheel size (20-inch diameter is standard; 24-inch wheels are known as "cruiser" class), by age, and by gender. Freestyle competitions focus more on tricks and jumps than on speed.

★ **WHERE TO PLAY AND WATCH:**

BMX is a year-round sport, and local clubs offer open race days throughout the year for curious fans. At the professional level in the United States, the two main sanctioning bodies—the National Bicycle League (NBL; www.nbl.org) and the American Bicycle Association (ABA; www.ababmx.com)—organize local, regional, and national races. The latter is also recognized by the sport's international governing body, the International Cycling Union (UCI; www.uci.ch).

MOUNTAIN BIKING

----- GOING DOWNHILL FAST -----

IF YOU THINK THE GROWTH CURVE OF BMX is uniquely impressive, think again. Off-road biking, or mountain biking, is another of those rare sports that went from nonexistent to full-medal Olympic sport in fewer than three decades. Mountain biking has been contested at the Olympics since 1996.

Mountain biking was invented in the 1970s just outside San Francisco, in the hills of adjacent Marin County. The first mountain bike race was held in 1976 on a two-mile trail with a descent of more than 1,300 feet. Needless to say, the sport was not easy on street bikes of the era. This forced the sport's early enthusiasts to innovate, in the process creating an entirely new class of bicycle brandishing some serious performance enhancements (dual suspension, lightweight frames, upward-tilting handlebars, disc brakes, traction tires). Today's mountain bikes are true technological marvels.

★ **BASIC CONCEPT:**

There are numerous competitive classes of mountain bike racing. Cross-country (the category contested at the Olympics) is an indivi-dual competition with massed starts and tracks covering 45 to 50 kilometers. Downhill racing, also an individual competition, is a time-trial event, with riders starting at intervals and competing for the lowest overall times.

ROAD RACING

----- STRIVE FOR THE YELLOW JERSEY -----

ROAD RACING IS THE OLDEST FORM OF BICYCLE RACING—it dates back to the earliest days of the bicycle itself. The very first world championship was held in 1893 and road racing has been a medal sport at every summer Olympics since 1896. Some of the sport's oldest races are still hotly contested today, including the Tour de France (established in 1903) and the Giro d'Italia (established in 1909).

Individual time trials are a common race format, and racers compete for both individual and team standings. Yet when most people think of road racing they think of team tour events such as the Tour de France, with small groups of cyclists competing for the overall best times and alternating riders leading different legs of the race based on their riding specialties.

★ **BASIC CONCEPT:**

Road races are run on mixed terrain, from city streets to steep mountain passes. In team races, riders invariably employ the tactic of "drafting" whereby a trailing rider (or riders) slips into position behind other riders to conserve energy (a drafting rider can save up to 35 percent of their energy this way). Drafting is less effective on climbs, as the low speeds reduce the efficiency of the forward drafting motion.

Riders are usually selected by teams for their individual specialties: climber, sprinter, domestique (a rider with the specific job of assisting the team leader or leaders), and time trialist (a rider who can maintain high speeds for extended periods).

THE WORLD'S MOST FAMOUS ROAD-RACING EVENT *has distinct ways of honoring its top riders. During the race, the overall time leader (lowest overall time for all completed stages) wears the prestigious yellow jersey.*

A green jersey is awarded to the race's points leader (points are awarded for finishing first, second, and third during individual stages, for top sprint times, etc., and subtracted for any penalties doled out by race officials).

A white jersey with red dots is awarded to riders who are first to climb preselected hills and mountain passes, while a plain white jersey is awarded to the best young rider (under age twenty-six).

Believe it or not, there's also an award (no jersey— just bragging rights) doled out to the tour's most com- bative rider (the so-called Prix de la Combativité) and the tour's slowest rider (the "lanterne rouge," often symbolized by a red light hanging beneath the unlucky rider's seat).

★ **WHERE TO PLAY AND WATCH:**

Road racing is mainly a spring and summer sport, with a busy calendar of racing events (both amateur and professional) from March through September. The sport's three "grand tours" are the Tour de France, Italy's Giro d'Italia, and Spain's Vuelta a España. Road racing's governing body, the International Cycling Union (UCI; www.uci.ch), sponsors pro tours in numerous countries, while national bodies, including USA Cycling (www.usacycling.org), host races and time trials throughout the year.

TRACK CYCLING

----- MEET YOU AT THE VELODROME -----

TRACK CYCLING IS THE IDEAL BLEND OF PRESTIGE (the sport has been around since the 1880s and appeared at all but one Olympics since 1896) and flat-out insanity (the racing action is fast and furious). The eponymous "track" can be the outdoor variety or, more commonly, an indoor oval known as a velodrome. Modern indoor tracks are 250 meters in circumference and steeply banked at both ends (to a massive angle of 45 degrees). This has the effect of bunching racers at the bottom edge of the track except when lagging riders attempt to pass a rider in front, first surging forward and up the angled track before leaning with gravity and rocketing back down the track face as fast as possible.

No surprise that track cycling is all about aerodynamics. Both individual and team track cyclists "draft" off one another to take advantage of the reduced energy required to keep pace when following in the slipstream of a leading rider. Track bikes are also highly evolved: lightweight carbon-fiber frames with airfoil designs reduce drag as much as possible.

Track bikes have only one gear and racers must decide whether to optimize for quick acceleration (using a lower gear) or sustained speed (using a higher gear). The gearing decision often comes down to what type of event the racer is contesting.

★ BASIC CONCEPT:

Track cycling is generally divided into sprint and endurance races, with head-to-head racing formats (first across the finish line wins) plus individual and team time-trials (lowest overall times win). Sprint races last between three and nine laps and put the focus on quick acceleration and sprinting prowess. Endurance races are much longer, anywhere from twelve to two hundred laps.

Equestrian Sports

CHAPTER NINE

HORSE RACING

HORSES WERE DOMESTICATED SOMETIME AROUND 4000 BC. It's a safe bet to say horse racing (and betting on horse racing) started about ten minutes later. Most of the great civilizations on earth have raced horses in some fashion, be it the Greeks, Chinese, Celts, or Romans. In the United States the first purpose-built track dates from the late 1600s, and by 1900 there were literally hundreds of established horse-racing tracks from coast to coast. The rule of thumb seems to be where there are people and horses, there is horse racing.

5 MOST FAMOUS THOROUGHBRED
HORSES OF ALL TIME

★ **AFFIRMED.**
He is the most recent Triple Crown winner (1978) and only the eleventh horse ever to win the prestigious "Crown."

★ **BLACK GOLD.**
Won the 1924 Kentucky Derby but only because his owner, Al Hoots, had had a deathbed vision to breed his mare, U-See-It, with a competitor's stallion. Six years later Al's widow validated her husband's vision at the 1924 Kentucky Derby.

★ **MAN O' WAR.**
He raced twenty-one times and lost only once. Enough said.

★ **SECRETARIAT.**
He was the 1973 Triple Crown winner and is credited with reviving interest in horse racing in the United States. He won the 1973 Belmont Stakes by an unbelievable thirty-one lengths.

★ **SKIP AWAY.**
He won sixteen stakes events over a four-year racing career and is one of the leading money earners of all time, capturing $9 million in career race earnings.

★ THOROUGHBRED RACING: BASIC CONCEPT

The most common type of horse race is the Thoroughbred. The name refers to an actual breed of horse, and all Thoroughbred horses can trace their lineage back to a small handful of mares and stallions imported from the Arabian Peninsula to England in the seventeenth century. With an *average* auction value of around $100,000, Thoroughbred horses are extraordinarily valuable due to centuries of selective breeding targeting speed, strength, and stamina.

In the United States the most famous Thoroughbred races are the so-called Triple Crown events of the Kentucky Derby, the Preakness Stakes, and the Belmont Stakes. The Breeders' Cup races round out the elite racing calendar. Thoroughbred races are run on dirt (occasionally turf) and last anywhere from five to twelve furlongs (the traditional horse-racing measurement, equivalent to one-eighth of a mile or about 220 yards). Horse jockeys play a subtle but crucial role guiding the horse around the track and deciding when to lay back or be aggressive as they literally jockey for best position.

★ QUARTER HORSE RACING: BASIC CONCEPT

This race is named after the American Quarter Horse, a breed purposefully selected to run very, very fast. Quarter Horse races are run, as the name implies, on quarter-mile tracks with no turns or curves. Horses run at top speed the entire way, and jockeys have less overall influence on the race outcomes. This sport is all about fast horses.

★ STEEPLECHASE: BASIC CONCEPT

This style of racing mimics a race in the open countryside; the sport's name refers to races run from church steeple to church steeple, or town to town. Steeplechase tracks feature all sorts of obstacles (streams, ponds, open ditches) and fences or posts for jumping. Steeplechase events have multiple riders competing head to head, which makes the sport exciting to watch.

★ **HARNESS RACING: BASIC CONCEPT**

Think of the classic Greek or Roman chariot race, minus the spears and swords, and you've got the basic concept of harness racing. The modern version attaches a two-wheeled cart, called a sulky or a bike, to the back of a standardbred horse (a breed with shorter legs, and less spirit, than Thoroughbreds). Races are run at two speeds (trotting or pacing) and cover distances of one mile. The drivers (please, don't call them jockeys) are crucial factors in managing the horse's gait and overall racing strategy. Harness racing requires more human strategy than all other types of horse racing.

OLYMPIC COMPETITIONS

----- THE TESTS OF A TRUE EQUESTRIAN -----

EQUESTRIAN EVENTS WERE INCLUDED in the Olympics as early as 1900 and have been full-medal events in every games since 1912. Riders compete in three categories: dressage, jumping, and eventing. All three categories feature solo and team competitions, and all three feature men and women competing directly against one another (a mixed-gender rarity at the Olympics).

★ **DRESSAGE: BASIC CONCEPT**

The word *dressage* roughly means "training" in French and refers to the effortless control of a horse by its rider. Dressage competitions feature highly trained horses acting as naturally as possible, responding to the subtle commands of their rider as both rider and horse perform a suite of predetermined tests showcasing their talents. Typical dressage displays include trots, canters, pirouettes, and half-passes (where the horse moves diagonally forward and sideways at the same time). Riders are scored on a scale from 0 (not performed) to 10 (excellent), and the rider or team with the highest overall score wins the events.

★ EVENTING: BASIC CONCEPT

This is a multidisciplinary event held over the course of three or four days. Generally days one and two feature dressage competitions, day three is usually dedicated to a cross-country, and day four is given over to show jumping. Cross-country is an event showcasing endurance, with a series of fences and natural obstacles (thirty to forty in total) laid out over a long circuit and interspersed with ponds and ditches to mimic a ride in the countryside. Riders earn points by clearing all the obstacles and riding the course under an optimum time. Riders are eliminated if they fall anywhere along the course.

★ SHOW JUMPING: BASIC CONCEPT

Riders navigate the horse through a series of jumps, competing against a clock and attempting to score as few faults or penalties as possible. Scores are based solely on the horse's ability to clear an obstacle and finish the course on time. Show jumping courses generally feature a dozen or more different jumps in a set order.

POLO

----- EIGHT HORSES CHASING AFTER ONE TINY BALL -----

POLO IS ANOTHER ANCIENT SPORT, with references going as far back as the fifth century BC. The birthplace of polo is disputed, but certainly modern Iran is on the short list (the king and queen of Persia played head-to-head polo matches in the sixth century AD). Pakistan and India, too, were early adopters of polo. The British imported polo from India in the 1860s. Today polo is played professionally in at least fourteen countries including the United States.

★ **BASIC CONCEPT**

Two teams, each fielding four riders on horseback, attempt to score by swinging mallets (long sticks, resembling croquet mallets) and knocking a small white ball into their opponent's goal. Polo teams change direction after every goal. Polo fields are usually 300 by 160 to 200 yards, more than three times as large as American football fields and giving teams plenty of room to maneuver the horses. The pace of the game is similar to ice hockey, with frequent shifts from offense to defense. Games last from four to six chukkers (periods), with each period lasting 7½ minutes.

★ **RULES AND TERMINOLOGY**

Polo goals are usually 8 yards wide, and one point is scored by hitting the ball between the posts (no matter how high). Professional matches are overseen by three umpires: two mounted umpires who follow the on-field action, and one umpire sitting at midfield.

Whistles indicate fouls (generally for unsafe play). An especially flagrant foul draws a penalty shot from 30, 40, or 60 yards or from midfield.

★ **WHERE TO PLAY AND WATCH**:

The United States Polo Association (USPA; www.us-polo.org) organizes local and regional tournaments across the USA from Honolulu to Santa Barbara, Detroit to Des Moines, Houston to Saratoga.

VARIANT » ARENA POLO

Arena (indoor) polo is a less fussy, more accessible way to play and watch polo. The rules are similar to traditional polo, the main differences being the number of players (three per team, instead of four) and the size of the playing field (100 by 50 yards, instead of 300 by 200 yards). Arena polo is a slower game, but also a more physical one given the tighter spaces involved. In arena polo, teams switch ends at the end of each chukker and not after a goal is scored.

RODEO RIDING

----- IT'S ALL BOOTS, CHAPS, AND COWBOY HATS -----

RODEOS ARE A HIGHLY COMPETITIVE VENUE for showcasing the skills required of a traditional cowboy or ranch hand. Rodeos are a popular spectator sport in the USA, Canada, parts of South America, and even down under in Australia. Events are held for both men and women, and are typically divided into the timed events (roping, barrel racing, and steer wrestling) and the so-called "rough stock" events that are more about staying in the saddle as the bucking bronco tries to knock its rider off.

★ **BARREL RACING: BASIC CONCEPT**

This popular rodeo event is primarily for women, at least at the professional level. Female riders compete for the best time riding a cloverleaf pattern around a fixed obstacle course of three barrels. The barrels are arranged in the shape of a large triangle, and riders must manage their horses with precision.

Competitions feature a running start, with the rider and horse entering the racing area at top speed. The clock starts and stops when the horse crosses the starting and finishing lines. If a rider knocks or touches a barrel, 5 seconds are added to their time. Riders are disqualified if they completely miss a turn around a barrel.

★ **BRONC AND BULL RIDING: BASIC CONCEPT**

These two "rough stock" events are incredibly dangerous and require strength, skill, and endurance. Bronc riding comes in two varieties—

BEST RODEO SONG LYRICS (EVER)

Like your country music raunchy and served up with a heaping spoonful of dry prairie wit? Meet Garry Lee and Showdown. This Canadian fiddle and gee-tar band penned one of country music's most notorious rodeo odes on the 1980 album *Welcome to the Rodeo*. Crank up the volume next time you're practicing the two-step or chapping up.

Well it's forty below and I don't give a fuck
Got a heater in my truck and I'm off to the rodeo
And it's allemande left allemande right
Come on ya fuckin' dummy get your right step right

—*"THE RODEO SONG"*

bareback and saddle—and in both cases features a rider attempting to stay on a bucking horse for as long as possible before completing a ride or being thrown off. Bull riding is essentially the same, except the bronco is replaced by a full-grown bull.

Two non-competing bullfighters are always present in the ring, to assist riders who fall and to distract a bull from attacking its fallen rider.

★ ROPING: BASIC CONCEPT

Rodeos usually feature two different roping competitions: calf roping and team roping. The former is a timed event where a rider on a horse must lasso a running calf, dismount from the horse, and tie up three of the calf's legs, as quickly as possible. Team roping, on

the other hand, features two riders (a "header" and a "heeler") and a steer. The goal is for the header to rope the steer's head or horns and the heeler to rope the steer's hind legs. A penalty is given if only one leg is roped. Interestingly, team roping is the only rodeo event where men and women compete together.

★ STEER WRESTLING: BASIC CONCEPT

This is easily the most physically demanding event in a rodeo. The point of steer wrestling is for a rider to gallop up alongside a mature steer weighing around 500 pounds, grab its horns, jump off the horse, and then wrestle the steer to the ground. Once the steer's four legs no longer touch the ground, the steer is released and the rider's time is recorded (professional steer wrestlers can accomplish this feat in as few as three seconds!). The rider who legally wrestles a steer to the ground in the shortest amount of time wins the competition.

VAULTING

----- GYMNASTICS ON HORSEBACK -----

THE SPORT OF VAULTING HAS ANCIENT ROOTS: people have performed feats of balance from horseback for more than two thousand years! Today, spectators's experience of vaulting is limited to the circus or rodeo, where costumed gymnasts and dancers perform acrobatic moves from the back of a horse moving at full canter. Vaulting was an Olympics demonstration sport in 1984 and 1996.

★ **BASIC CONCEPT:**

Vaulting competitions feature solo, pair, and team riders covering a set of compulsory exercises designed to demonstrate the skill of both rider(s) and horse. Horses are attached to a trainer (the "longuer") by a long rein and move in 45-foot circles. Vaulters are judged on how well they perform the set exercises (basic seat, flag, mill, scissors, stand, and flank) as well as on their mount and dismount. In team events, every vaulter must complete all six exercises. In freestyle competitions, music and choreography are added to the mix, and vaulters are allowed more freedom to incorporate mounts, dismounts, kneeling, handstands, and even flips as part of the routine.

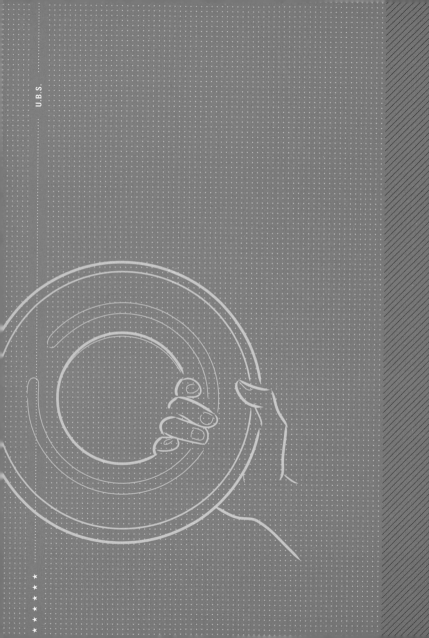

★ ⋯⋯ **10** ⋯⋯ ★

Fictional Sports

CHAPTER TEN

TERRESTRIAL SPORTS

----- LIVING IN AN OVERPOPULATED DYSTOPIA SUCKS THE FUN -----
OUT OF MOST SPORTS

GATHER FILM AND NOVEL WRITERS TOGETHER (possibly with a bottle of tequila or some medicinal marijuana) and there's no limit to the odd—and downright brutal—sport concepts that will end up on screen or in books. What's unique about this chapter is that the following fictional sports have earthly analogs you could actually play. Sorta.

★ **BASEKETBALL: BASIC CONCEPT**

This sport comes from the 1998 film of the same name, starring *South Park* creators Matt Stone and Trey Parker (as well as Ernest Borgnine—extra points for casting!). The idea is simple, in a totally stupid way: start with baseball, but instead of hitting a ball with a stick, movement around the bases is governed by whether or not players can sink a basketball shot. Free throws are a single, a shot from the top of the key is a double, and three-pointers are triples. No running required, so it's an ideal sport for the morbidly obese basketball fanatic. Strategy tip? Use profanity liberally. It's not just encouraged, it's required.

Best line from the movie: "Hey pigfucker, can I call you pigfucker?"

★ **DEATH RACE: BASIC CONCEPT**

The 1975 film *Death Race 2000* stars Sly Stallone and David Carradine, another brilliant casting decision. The eponymous Death Race involves driving whacked-out cars across the USA, earning points by smashing into people (extra points for old people and babies). Death Race fans help their favorite drivers rack up points by sacrificing themselves, too.

Best line from the movie: "Well America, there you have it, Frankenstein has just been attacked by the French Air Force and he's whipped their derrieres!"

★ **FUTURESPORT: BASIC CONCEPT**

The 1998 made-for-television movie *Futuresport* gets the blame for this inane sporting concept (not even Wesley Snipes and Vanessa Williams can save the script). Futuresport is a hybrid of baseball, basketball, and hockey—using in-line skates and skateboards—that's meant to lure the world's most deadly gang members off the street. Complications arise when world peace is threatened by terrorists from the Hawaiian Liberation Organization. C'mon, people, for real?

Best line from the movie: "On behalf of my gang, the North American Alliance, I challenge you to a game of Futuresport. The winner gets respect, bragging rights, and the Hawaiian Islands to boot."

★ **GUMBALL RALLY: BASIC CONCEPT**

This classic 1976 film features a coast-to-coast rally race by drivers who only need to have the word "gumball" whispered in their ear to hit the road in souped-up street cars. It's an old-school car race, full of gentle shenanigans and a gumball machine trophy for the winners.

Best line from the movie: "And now my friend, the first-a rule of Italian driving. What's-a behind me is not important."

★ **JUGGER: BASIC CONCEPT**

What, you've never heard of the 1989 movie *The Blood of Heroes*? Tsk tsk. It's the one with Rutger Hauer *and* Vincent D'Onofrio. The movie is a complete downer and utterly forgettable, except for the fact that it outlines very specific rules to a sport called jugger. The object? To place a dog skull (called the "jugg") on the opposing team's stake in the ground. Only one player from each team can touch the skull; he's called the "qwik." Also on the field is a player called the "chain" (armed with a chain weapon) and three "enforcers" (each brandishing swords and pikes). The chain and enforcers are there to beat the hell out of the other team's qwik. Vincent, seriously, what were you thinking?

Best line from the movie: "This is stupid. We should be fucking and drinking by now."

★ **ROLLERBALL: BASIC CONCEPT**

Oh how we miss you, Moonpie. The idea of this awesome 1975 movie is that, in the future, corporations have replaced all governments and use the sport of rollerball to control the masses. Rollerball itself is played by teams on roller skates and motorcycles (yes!) attempting to throw a magnetized steel ball into a metal goal. Murdering one's opponents is encouraged.

Strategy tip? Don't put your head in front of the cannon that fires the steel ball at the start of each possession.

Best line from the movie: "Ladies and gentlemen, will you stand please for the playing of our Corporate Hymn."

★   **RUNNING MAN: BASIC CONCEPT**

Steven King wrote the original story, and one can only wonder what he thinks about Arnold Schwarzenegger's performance in the 1987 film of the same name. "The Running Man" is the future's most popular game show, hosted by Richard Dawson (of course). In the future the economy has collapsed and the government attempts to quell people's yearning for freedom by broadcasting a game show in which convicted criminals have a chance to escape their sentences.

The catch? Contestants must evade government assassins for thirty days and send back daily video messages which are broadcast to a live studio audience. Few contestants survive, until Arnold shows up.

Best line from the movie: "I'll be back."

INTERSTELLAR AND MYTHICAL SPORTS

----- A LONG TIME AGO ON A BROOMSTICK FAR, FAR AWAY -----

OKAY, NOW TAKE THAT SAME BUNCH OF WHACKED-OUT WRITERS, put them in a dark room, and tell them to invent something completely different. Let the interstellar games begin!

★ **BROCKIAN ULTRA-CRICKET: BASIC CONCEPT**

Douglas Adams's book *The Hitchhiker's Guide to the Galaxy* includes the marvelously curious sport of Brockian Ultra-Cricket. Players should hit each other as hard as possible with cricket bats, basecube bats, tennis guns, skis, or anything that delivers a hearty, swinging smack. When a hit is scored on an opposing player, run far away and apologize from a safe distance. Apologies are scored by judges and "should be concise, sincere and, for maximum clarity and points, delivered through a megaphone." Unfortunately most teams who play Brockian Ultra-Cricket end up in a state of permanent warfare over the correct interpretation of the sport's rules.

★ **FLAMINGO CROQUET: BASIC CONCEPT**

Lewis Carroll was clearly unaware of organizations such as the SPCA when he created the sport of flamingo croquet in his book *Alice's Adventures in Wonderland*. The concept is wonderfully simple: it's like regular croquet, but uses flamingos for mallets. Play on.

★ **GERMAN BATBALL: BASIC CONCEPT**

Life on Mars would be tedious without German batball. The game was invented by Kurt Vonnegut in his novel *The Sirens of Titan*. The game plays like baseball with a few key twists: the ball is "the size of a big honeydew melon…and no more lively than a ten-gallon hat filled with rain water." Crucially, there is no bat. Players simply punch the ball with their fists.

★ **PODRACING: BASIC CONCEPT**

This illegal sport may be the only good thing about *Star Wars: Episode I—The Phantom Menace* (sorry, George, the truth hurts). Attach jet engines to an antigravity pod and let 'er rip! It's a high-speed race where anything goes. Avoid the obstacles and booby traps, not to mention the other podracers firing blasters willy-nilly at the competition, and your nonhuman pod driver might win everlasting glory. Until its head explodes, trying to escape.

★ **QUIDDITCH: BASIC CONCEPT**

The quintessential Harry Potter sport is an airborne combination of soccer, basketball, and hockey. Goals are scored by chucking a small ball called the quaffle through one of the opponent's three circular goals. A goal is worth 10 points. The quaffle has a spell cast on it, making it fall slowly through the air so that players don't have to continuously dive on their brooms to retrieve it. Players should also avoid the bludgers, large iron balls patrolling the pitch and knocking players off their brooms indiscriminately.

A quidditch match can end on a moment's notice if either team captures the golden snitch, a walnut-sized winged ball that makes unpredictable appearances during the match. The snitch is worth 150 points and each team has a designated "seeker" whose only job is to find and capture it.

Quidditch is another game that's made the jump from fiction to reality. Nobody's playing with jetpacks just yet, but more than three hundred universities and high schools in the United States have honest-to-goodness quidditch teams. They play a terrestrial version of the game under the auspices of the International Quidditch Association (IQA; www.internationalquidditch.org). Leading the rankings is Middlebury College, followed by Arizona State University and Louisiana State University.

★ **TRIAD: BASIC CONCEPT**

This one comes from the television series *Battlestar Galactica* (the original version). It's a contact sport with elements of football and basketball, played on a triangular court by two coed teams of two players. It's all the rage in the Twelve Colonies. A game begins with players holding hands (not kidding) and turning in a circle until the ball is ejected from one of the goals. From this point on the rules are vague, though clearly foreplay is at the bottom of it all.

It's the pentathlon of the future. Get sucked into a computer and don your glow-in-the-dark unitard in preparation for five different athletic  competitions courtesy of the 1982 film *Tron*. First up is Battle Tanks (tank in a maze, shoot everything). Next is I/O Tower (destroy weird bugs with discs, run to the flashing circle). Then there are Light Cycles (get your opponent to crash into your light trail, avoid their light trail) and Flying Frisbees (throw a glowing disc, fatally, at your opponents). And finally it's MCP Cone, battling the Master Control Program by knocking down its wall and jumping into, er, a cone.

★ **TSUNKATSE: BASIC CONCEPT**

Star Trek fans, don't worry, you're included, too. This version of kickboxing-cum-Japanese martial arts is played in several *Star Trek: Voyager* episodes. It's a lethal sport, with combatants wearing devices on their front and back that deliver a shock when touched by a device on their opponent's feet and hands.

11

Football and Rugby

CHAPTER ELEVEN

AMERICAN FOOTBALL

FOOTBALL IS THE MOST POPULAR SPORT IN THE UNITED STATES. And that's not including college football, which is a sporting industry in its own right and garners nearly as much television time as the professional version. The sport is also uniquely American. It's played nowadays in Europe, Japan, and Canada, but if we're being honest, the game of gridiron (football's long-standing nickname) has been tweaked and tuned to fit an American sensibility (and, crucially, American television schedules).

Without rugby, there would be no American football. Rugby was developed in England and brought to the United States in the mid-nineteenth century, where it thrived at American colleges and universities. But starting in the late 1890s many American universities began ditching their rugby programs in favor of the newly created sport of football, which featured novelties such as forward passing (illegal in rugby), teams of eleven (versus fifteen in rugby), and a system of fixed possession, called downs, built around a line of scrimmage (there are no downs in rugby). The University of California at Berkeley's rugby team, for example, was disbanded in 1885 in favor of football, brought back from 1906 to 1914 when football was considered too dangerous, and replaced by football a second time in 1914! The early years of American football were tumultuous.

The first professional football league was founded in 1903. The National Football League (NFL; www.nfl.com) was created in 1922. By 1958, when the first NFL championship game was broadcast nationally on the NBC television network, football had reached its popularity tipping point. Two years later the rival American Football League was founded, proving that Americans' appetite for football was strong enough to support two professional leagues. In 1966 the AFL agreed to merge with the NFL to create the first-ever Super Bowl, played by the winners of the newly created two-conference system: the American Football Conference (AFC), named in honor of the AFL, and the National Football Conference (NFC), named in honor of the NFL.

★ **BASIC CONCEPT**:

Two teams of eleven players compete to score points by running the football into, or catching a pass inside, the opponent's end zone; kicking the ball through the opponent's goal posts; or tackling an opposing player with possession of the ball in his own end zone.

★ ★ ★ ★ ★ ·········· U.B.S. ·········· ★ ★ ★ ★ ★

AMERICAN FOOTBALL

The team on offense (in possession of the ball) has four downs to score or move the ball a minimum of 10 yards toward the opponent's end zone. When the offense gains at least 10 yards on any play, they are immediately awarded four more downs. If they fail, the defensive team gains possession from where the fourth down ended.

Football games are divided into 15-minute quarters. Ties are decided in 15-minute, sudden-death overtime periods (play continues until a winner is declared). It used to be that games were won in overtime by the first team to score. In 2012 the NFL updated its rules and now both teams must have the opportunity to possess the ball at least once in overtime. The only exception is when the team receiving the overtime kickoff scores a touchdown (as opposed to a field goal) on its first possession.

★ **EQUIPMENT AND PLAYING SPACE:**

Football fields are 360 feet long by 160 feet wide. Goal lines at either end are exactly 100 yards apart, with end zones extending an additional 10 yards behind the goal lines. Inside the end zones, at the far

ends, two U-shaped goalposts stand 10 feet above the ground, with posts 18½ feet across. Yard lines cross the field every 5 yards and are labeled every 10 yards (starting from the 50-yard line at midfield and showing the distance to the closest goal line).

Footballs (also called pigskins, in dubious homage to the pigskin bladders once used to inflate footballs) are a foot long and 22 inches in circumference. Pointed ends make it easier—and faster—to throw the ball over long distances, an important feature in a game with forward passing.

★ **RULES AND TERMINOLOGY:**

Action on the field stops at the end of every play, giving both offense and defense a chance to call new plays, to adjust their position on the field, and to substitute players (football is an unlimited-substitution game, with players continuously coming on and off the field). Other important concepts in football include:

» **Line of scrimmage:** *This is an imaginary line drawn to mark where play begins. Opposing players cannot cross the line until the ball is in play. The scrimmage line is also important for passing: the offense can throw the ball forward only once per down and only from behind the line of scrimmage. (Lateral and reverse passes are allowed at any time.)*

» **Tackling:** *Football is a physical full-contact sport (note the mandatory pads and helmets). On every play the opposing teams face off across the line of scrimmage and collide once the ball is in play, in an attempt to control their position on the field. To stop a play the defense must knock the offensive ball carrier or quarterback out of bounds or tackle him to the ground, or disrupt the football in flight.*

» **Rushing, passing, punting:** *The quarterback is the offensive team's leader and play caller. The quarterback initiates a rushing (running) or passing play to move the ball down the field. If the offensive team is short of a first down they may elect to punt the ball, kicking it down the field for the other team to catch and return if possible.*

» **Turnovers:** *Teams can lose possession of the ball through a fumble (dropping or otherwise losing control of the ball) or interception (allowing the opposing team to catch and control a thrown football).*

» **Scoring:** *Teams score touchdowns (6 points) by running the ball into, or catching a pass inside, the opponent's end zone. After a touchdown the scoring team earns possession of the ball at the opponent's 2-yard line and can either kick an extra point (1 point) or attempt a two-point conversion (2 points). Teams can attempt a field goal (3 points) at any point during*

TOP 5 VINCE LOMBARDI QUOTES

VINCE LOMBARDI IS A FOOTBALL LEGEND. As coach of the Green Bay Packers in the 1960s, he led the team to three league championships and two Super Bowl wins (the Super Bowl's Lombardi trophy is named in his honor). Vince had a way with words, especially when it came to discussing his favorite topic: winning. Below are some of his most famous quotes:

★ *"If you can't accept losing, you can't win."*

★ *"Winning isn't everything, but wanting to win is."*

★ *"Winning is a habit. Unfortunately, so is losing."*

★ *"Practice does not make perfect. Only perfect practice makes perfect."*

★ *"If it doesn't matter who wins or loses, then why do they keep score?"*

their normal possession, often in lieu of scoring a touchdown. If an offensive player with possession of the ball is tackled in his own end zone, a safety (2 points) is scored.

» ***Penalties:*** *Common penalties in football include false starts (crossing the line of scrimmage before the ball is in play), illegal blocking or tackling, holding (illegal contact with a player not in possession of the ball), and pass interference (illegal contact with an intended receiver after the ball has been thrown but before it is caught). Most penalties result in replaying the down and moving the football 5, 10, or 15 yards towards the opposing team's end zone. When a foul occurs in the middle of a play, the referee marks it by throwing a yellow penalty flag.*

VARIANT » CANADIAN FOOTBALL

Football in Canada is quite similar to its American counterpart. The main differences are the number of players (Canadian football fields twelve players to American football's eleven) and the number of downs (three downs as opposed to four downs in American football). There are other subtler differences, too: Canadian footballs are more rounded at the ends, and players are allowed to drop-kick a ball (drop it on the field and kick it). Both are remnants of the sport's stronger rugby heritage.

RUGBY UNION

RUGBY UNION, OFTEN CALLED PLAIN OLD RUGBY, is one of two versions of rugby played today (the other is rugby league, which split and created its own sporting identity in 1895). The differences between the two are fairly minor (union fields fifteen players, league fields thirteen) and both share a common ancestry. Rugby was invented at the Rugby School in England in the 1840s.

Rugby's influence has since spread far and wide, with more than a hundred countries (especially within the British Commonwealth) fielding professional teams and national leagues. Rugby is also credited with inspiring football (the American gridiron version). After an absence of more than 90 years, rugby (in the form of rugby sevens) is set to be reinstated as a full-medal Olympic sport at the 2016 summer games.

★ **BASIC CONCEPT**:

Two teams of fifteen players compete to score points. Rugby does not have downs and play is continuous. The same team can retain possession until they score, lose possession, or have a penalty called. Players can run with the ball, pass the ball laterally or backwards (forward passes are illegal), or kick the ball up the field. There is no blocking in rugby, and only the player in possession of the ball can be tackled.

Teams score points by grounding the ball (i.e., touching the ball to the ground) in the in-goal area for a "try," worth 5 points; a successful conversion kick following a try is worth 2 additional points. Teams can score 3 points each for a successful penalty kick or a drop goal (when a player drop-kicks the ball over and through the goalposts that are positioned at both ends of the pitch). Games are divided into 40-minute halves. The team with the higher score wins and ties or draws are allowed (in major competitions, ties are settled by playing two 10-minute halves of extra time, if necessary followed by a 10-minute sudden-death period in which the first team to score wins).

★ EQUIPMENT AND PLAYING SPACE:

Rugby pitches measure a maximum 144 meters long by 70 meters wide. Two try lines (goal lines) are generally 100 meters apart, with up to 22 meters of "dead-ball area" behind the try lines (a ball is out of bounds beyond the dead-ball area). A halfway line is drawn at both ends of the pitch 22 meters from their respective try lines. Rugby goalposts are H-shaped with two poles set 5.6 meters apart and the crossbar set 3 meters above the ground. Rugby balls are oval with rounded ends (as opposed to the pointed ends of American-style footballs).

★ RULES AND TERMINOLOGY:

Rugby players are numbered 1 to 15, and the number signifies that player's position. Players 1 to 8 are forwards, typically large and strong, with the main job of winning possession of the ball from the opposing team. Players 9 to 15 are backs, typically smaller and faster, with the main job of taking advantage of balls won by their forwards. Other important concepts include:

> » **Continuous Play:** *Rugby play does not stop when the ball hits the ground, when a player is tackled, or even when a drop-kick misses the goalposts. When a player in possession of the ball is legally tackled, they must release the ball so that other players can play the ball.*

» **Scrum:** Referees whistle and halt play for minor penalties (such as when the ball has been knocked or passed forward, or when the ball is trapped in a ruck or maul [see below] and can't be played). Players form a scrum to restart play. Eight players from each team form adjacent lines, three rows deep, creating a sort of tunnel over the ball. The non-offending team (i.e., the team not responsible for trapping the ball) rolls the ball into the tunnel and both teams push forward until the players known as "hookers" are able to hook the ball with their feet. The hooker pushes the ball to the back of their side of the scrum. A player called the "scrum half" grabs the ball and play resumes.

» **Line Out:** Balls knocked out of bounds (called "in touch") are put back into play with a line out. Players from both teams stand 1 meter apart in lines perpendicular to the sideline. A player from the non-offending team (i.e., the team not responsible for knocking the ball out) steps out of bounds and, facing the pitch, throws the ball forward in the air, ideally in a straight line. The two lines of players then jump for the ball. It's perfectly legal for players to be lifted in the air by their teammates as they jump for possession.

» **Offside:** Similar to soccer, the ball in rugby forms an invisible line that prevents players from being on the opposing team's side of the ball. Just being offside is not a penalty; players must be offside and participating in the current play for an offside penalty to be called.

» **Ruck:** When a player is tackled and forced to let go of the ball, a ruck forms. Players from both teams converge over the free ball and form a human chain of sorts. The goal of the ruck is to push the opposing players backward, since the ball cannot be picked up until it emerges from the ruck. It's a huge advantage for the team that gains possession, since a ruck forms

FUN RUGBY FACTS

★ The world's oldest rugby club, established in 1854, is Dublin University Football Club.

★ Rugby is a popular women's sport and the international Women's Rugby World Cup is held every four years. New Zealand's women have dominated the competition since it started in 1991, winning four titles in a row. England and the USA each have one title.

★ A score is called a "try" because, originally, a try earned no points. Instead, a try earned the team a chance to kick a goal. The rules were changed over the years to boost scores and make the game more entertaining.

★ Rugby balls are oval because they were originally fashioned from pig bladders, which took a rounded shape when inflated.

- ★ Rugby union only went professional in 1995. Prior to that, the sport was for amateurs only (a polite way of saying, players were not paid).

- ★ Rugby was an Olympic sport in 1900, 1908, 1920, and 1924. The United States won the gold medal in both 1920 and 1924.

- ★ What do these people all have in common: Sean Connery, J.R.R. Tolkien, John F. Kennedy, George W. Bush, and Bill Clinton? Yup, they all played rugby.

offset lines—all players must get back in position to avoid an offside penalty, creating precious space on the field for the team in possession to move the ball forward.

» **Maul:** *A maul is like a ruck, except that the player in possession of the ball is not brought fully to the ground by his tackler. A maul is set once any three players are entangled around the ball. An offside line is formed by the feet of the last players on each side of the ball, and players from each team must quickly retreat behind the offside line in order to take part in the subsequent play. A maul ends once the ball emerges.*

» **Penalties:** *Free kicks are awarded for minor rule violations. Players cannot attempt to kick a goal; they can only kick the ball back into play. Penalty kicks are awarded for semi-serious rule violations. The offending team must retreat 10 meters and allow the other team to restart play unopposed. For repeated or serious violations players can be shown a yellow card and be sent off for 10 minutes, or shown a red card and sent off for the remainder of the game. In both cases the offending team plays a man down.*

★ **WHERE TO PLAY AND WATCH:**

Rugby union's governing body is the International Rugby Board (IRB; www.irb.com). The IRB sponsors the premier event in the sport, the Rugby World Cup. It's held every four years and, believe it or not, is rated as one of the largest international sporting event in the world after soccer's World Cup.

This seven-a-side version of rugby union follows essentially the same rules. The few changes that do exist are all intended to make the teams play faster and score more points. Halves are 7 minutes long (instead of 40 minutes), which makes it possible to organize a multi-team competition over a single day.

For all these reasons, rugby sevens was chosen by the International Olympic Committee (IOC) to represent rugby when the sport makes its reappearance at the Olympics in 2016. Rugby sevens is governed by the IRB.

RUGBY LEAGUE

----- IT'S BIG IN AUSTRALIA -----

RUGBY LEAGUE SPLIT FROM THE ORIGINAL SPORT of rugby (later rechristened rugby union) in 1895 over an argument about—what else—money. Since the split, both versions of the sport have evolved distinct rules and identities (though if we're being totally honest, the differences are minor).

The most obvious difference is the number of players on the field: union teams field fifteen players, league teams field thirteen. Fewer players mean a faster, more wide-open match in theory. Another notable difference is scoring. In union it's 5 points for a try, 3 points for a penalty goal, and 3 points for a drop goal. In league the corresponding points are 4, 2, and 1.

League is also more lenient when it comes to tackling. It's allowed to charge the player in possession and hit them hard with a shoulder. This leads to some seriously hard-hitting tackles and is the main reason league is considered the more physical of the two games.

Unlike in union, play stops in league when a player in possession is tackled. League teams also have the six-tackle rule (similar to "downs" in American football). The team in possession has six tackles to score; after the sixth tackle possession of the ball changes sides.

Finally, league fields are slightly smaller and look a lot like American football fields, thanks to the line markings spaced every 10 meters.

★ **WHERE TO PLAY AND WATCH:**

Rugby league's governing body is the Rugby League International Federation (RLIF; www.rlif.org). The RLIF administers the sport's two major international competitions, the Rugby League World Cup (won nine times by Australia!) and the Four Nations tournament, which actually comprises five teams (Australia, New Zealand, England, France, and one team from other Rugby League nations).

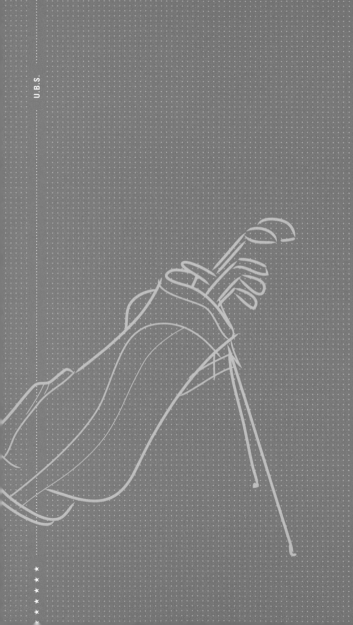

12

Golf

CHAPTER TWELVE

STROKE PLAY

----- "SEX AND GOLF ARE THE TWO THINGS YOU CAN ENJOY -----
EVEN IF YOU'RE NOT GOOD AT THEM."
—*KEVIN COSTNER IN* TIN CUP *(1996)*

THE OLD ADAGE SAYS GOLF IS EASY TO LEARN, but maddeningly hard to play well. That's partly because golf is an individual as opposed to a team sport, unlike nearly every other mainstream sport in the USA. As with any individual sport, it takes time to develop golf skills and most golfers are not willing to invest the time to get better. Golf is a commitment. Anybody can shoot hoops or play catch for a few minutes in the backyard, but playing golf requires expensive equipment and a minimum of 3½ to 4½ hours to play a complete 18-hole game.

Stick-and-ball games have existed for millennia, but the Scots are generally credited with inventing a game called "gouf" played over 18 holes. The game's first written reference is from an act of Scottish Parliament in the 1450s prohibiting the playing of golf (apparently it was a distraction from archery practice!). The world's first 18-hole course was pioneered at Scotland's Royal and Ancient Golf Club of St. Andrews, which is considered the "home of golf" and, along with the Honourable Company of Edinburgh Golfers, is one of the oldest established golf clubs.

Worldwide there are more than two dozen professional golf associations and tours, most notably the USA's Professional Golfers' Association (PGA; www.pga.com) and Ladies Professional Golfers' Association (LPGA; www.lpga.com). Both of these organize professional tours, as do their European counterparts. Golf's four major men's championships are the Masters, U.S. Open, British Open, and the PGA Championship. Uniquely among major golf tournaments, the Masters is played every year at the same course (Augusta National Golf Club, in Georgia).

Golf is also scheduled to be played at the 2016 Summer Olympics. The event will feature professional golfers as well as amateurs, guaranteeing a massive worldwide audience.

★ **BASIC CONCEPT**:

Golf is conceptually straightforward. Players use a variety of clubs to strike a small hard ball, with the goal of playing the ball in the fewest number of strokes from tee box (where golfers tee off, or commence hitting) to putting green (a manicured section at the end of every hole) and into the hole. A round of golf is 18 holes. Courses with 9 holes are common, in which case players make two circuits to complete a round.

✦ ✦ ✦ ✦ ✦ ✦ ·········· U.B.S. ·········· ✦ ✦ ✦ ✦ ✦ ✦

STROKE PLAY

In stroke play, golfers compete for the lowest overall score in a round or rounds (major golf championships typically play four rounds of 18 holes and sum players' scores from each round). A playoff round is used in case of ties. Playoffs either are sudden-death (lowest score wins the hole and the match) or are played over a predetermined number of holes (lowest total score wins).

★ **EQUIPMENT AND PLAYING SPACE:**

Golf is unique among major sports in that there are no standards governing the size, shape, or features of a golf course. That said,

the standard length is 9 or 18 holes, each with a tee box offset by markers showing the teeing area's legal boundaries. Holes typically all have three features: fairways (area between tee box and putting green with cut grass), roughs (area between fairway and out-of-bounds markers, with uncut grass and other obstacles), and putting greens (area of short grass with a flagstick or pin and a cup). Holes are graded on the average number of strokes (called par) required to hit a ball into the hole; almost universally holes are graded par 3 (250 yards or less), par 4 (251 to 450 yards), or par 5 (451 to 690 yards).

Courses may include hazards such as sand traps and water obstacles to enhance the overall level of difficulty. Links courses are built on top of sandy soil, usually on or near a coastline.

Golf balls are made of hard plastic with a rubber core. A dimpled exterior improves aerodynamics and increases the length balls will fly through the air. In competition play, balls must have a diameter less than 1.68 inches and cannot weigh more than 1.62 ounces.

TOP 10 GOLF QUOTES

★ "Golf is so popular simply because it is the best game in the world at which to be bad."
—*A. A. MILNE*

★ "Golf is a game that is played on a five-inch course— the distance between your ears."
—*BOBBY JONES*

★ "If a lot of people gripped a knife and fork the way they do a golf club, they'd starve to death."
—*SAM SNEAD*

★ "If you're caught on a golf course during a storm and are afraid of lightning, hold up a 1-iron. Not even God can hit a 1-iron."
—*LEE TREVINO*

★ "A perfectly straight shot with a big club is a fluke."
—*JACK NICKLAUS*

- ★ "Golf can best be defined as an endless series of tragedies obscured by the occasional miracle."
  —*ANONYMOUS*

- ★ "Don't be too proud to take a lesson. I'm not."
  —*JACK NICKLAUS*

- ★ "Why am I using a new putter? Because the old one didn't float too well."
  —*CRAIG STADLER*

- ★ "No matter how bad you are playing, it is always possible to play worse."
  —*ANONYMOUS*

- ★ "Just be the ball, be the ball, be the ball. You're not being the ball, Danny."
  —*CHEVY CHASE, FROM* CADDYSHACK *(1980)*

GOLF'S MOST WINNING PLAYERS

IN MEN'S GOLFING, the players with the most major championships are Jack Nicklaus, Tiger Woods, Walter Hagen, Gary Player, and Ben Hogan. The players with the most overall PGA tour wins are Sam Snead, Jack Nicklaus, Tiger Woods, Ben Hogan, and Arnold Palmer.

On the women's side the players with the most LPGA tour wins are Kathy Whitworth, Mickey Wright, Annika Sörenstam, Patty Berg, and Louise Suggs.

★ **RULES AND TERMINOLOGY:**

On longer par 4 and 5 holes, players typically use a large-faced club called a driver to hit the ball as far as possible. This stroke is called a drive. For second shots as well as tee shots on shorter holes, players use lighter clubs with smaller hitting faces called irons (numbered from 2-iron to 9-iron depending on the degree of angle of the club's hitting face). There are many hitting styles—pitch, chip, layup, approach—depending on where the ball lies, distance from ball to putting green, and potential obstacles between golfer and putting green. Once on the putting green, players use a narrow-faced club called a putter to knock the ball into the hole.

The official rules of golf are set by the Royal and Ancient Golf Club of St. Andrews and, in the United States, by the U.S. Golf Association (USGA; www.usga.org). Probably the most important rules are penalties for hitting the ball out of bounds or into unplayable rough.

In both cases players take a one-stroke penalty and remove the ball from the hazard, teeing it up behind the hazard where possible (or moving the ball to the nearest section of fairway).

Players must always hit the ball from where it lies. Players are not allowed to move or clear obstacles on the course, except on the putting green. In nonprofessional matches, it's tradition to allow every player one mulligan (an extra stroke allowed after a poor shot on the first tee box, not counted on the scorecard) per game.

At the end of each hole, golfers write down their individual scores on a scorecard. Common terms for scores include albatross (3 strokes under par), eagle (2 strokes under), birdie (1 stroke under), bogey (1 over par), double bogey (2 over par), triple bogey (3 over par), and snowman (the dreaded 8).

VARIANT » MATCH PLAY

The rules are nearly identical to stroke play, except that two players (or teams) compete for the lowest score on each hole. The lowest score wins the hole (ties result in split holes). A match play tournament is won by the player or team that wins the most holes (regardless of their total score in strokes).

VARIANT » SKINS

This is standard stroke play, but with the added incentive of gambling! Players compete for the lowest overall scores, but also play a separate match-style contest, with the player with the lowest score on each hole winning a prize (usually money). When players tie, the prize is rolled over to the next hole.

13

★ ⋯⋯ ★

Gymnastics

CHAPTER THIRTEEN

ARTISTIC

----- IT'S ALL ABOUT BALANCE -----

ARTISTIC GYMNASTICS IS THE MOST POPULAR and well-known of the three branches of the gymnastics family (rhythmic and trampoline gymnastics being the other two branches). Its popularity no doubt stems from the variety of its routines, and the competitive drama generated by powerhouse gymnastics nations such as Russia (and its predecessor, the Soviet Union), Romania, China, and the United States. A ticket to the gymnastics team finals remains one of the hottest tickets going at any Olympics.

Men and women do not compete against each other in artistic gymnastics, and in fact the genders perform different events in competition. For the women it's uneven parallel bars, balance beam, floor exercise, and vault. For the men it's floor, pommel horse, rings, vault, parallel bars, and horizontal bar. At the Olympics, gymnasts compete in up to four different categories: team qualifying and finals, all-around finals (gymnasts compete head-to-head and the top three performers earn medals), and apparatus finals (the best eight gymnasts in each skill compete for medals).

★ **BALANCE BEAM: BASIC CONCEPT**

The balance beam is literally that—a sturdy plank of wood measuring just 16 feet long and 4½ inches wide. The beam stands just over 4 feet above the ground and has a light spring to it, to make it less punishing on gymnasts' bodies. Female gymnasts (men do not perform on the balance beam) perform choreographed routines demonstrating acrobatic skills such as leaps, jumps, 360-degree turns on one foot, and 180-degree leg splits. Individual routines can last up to 90 seconds. Gymnasts earn points for completing the required elements of the routine, and for their mounts and dismounts. It's an automatic half-point deduction if a gymnast falls from the beam during a routine.

★ **FLOOR EXERCISE: BASIC CONCEPT**

Men and women both compete on the same spring-loaded, 40-by-40-foot floor. What's different is the accompanying music: men do not use music, women *always* use it. Otherwise the men's and women's routines are very similar. Both demonstrate strength and balance through tumbles, jumps, backward jumps, handstands, and turns. Gymnasts must also touch each corner of the mat at least once during their routine. For men the floor routine lasts no longer than 70 seconds. For women it's 90 seconds.

★ HORIZONTAL BAR: BASIC CONCEPT

The horizontal or high bar stands more than 9 feet above the padded floor, offering male gymnasts (women do not compete in this event) a platform for swings, twists, release-and-grip acrobatics, changes in direction, and high-speed aerial dismounts. The horizontal bar is one of the fastest-moving in terms of the speeds gymnasts can achieve as they swing around the bar. Routines start with an assist so the gymnast can reach the bar; then the acrobatics begin. Gymnasts grip the bar in different ways depending on the specific skill being demonstrated.

★ PARALLEL BARS: BASIC CONCEPT

This is another men-only event. Gymnasts compete on two parallel bars measuring 11½ feet in length, spaced no more than shoulder-width apart (between 17 and 20½ inches) and elevated 6½ feet above the floor. Gymnasts are required to display a suite of skills including hanging, swinging, upper-arm positions, handstands, pirouettes, under-swings, and a dismount—all the while moving to a constant rhythm (and losing points if the rhythm is broken).

★ POMMEL HORSE: BASIC CONCEPT

A pommel horse is a strange-looking contraption that makes sense when you know its historical context. The pommel horse was

developed in the 1700s to help cavalry soldiers learn how to mount and dismount their horses. As such, pommel horse routines stress leg work including scissors, straddles, and double-leg swinging circles. Dismounts are also critical and require a handstand element (usually passing through a handstand on the way to dismounting). Gymnasts must keep their feet pointed and legs straight throughout their routine.

★ RINGS: BASIC CONCEPT

This men-only exercise requires a phenomenal amount of upper-body strength. Gymnasts perform from two freely hanging hand rings, with the idea being that as the gymnast moves the rings don't swing and instead stay relatively fixed. Gymnasts may bring their bodies to an L-shaped sitting position, swing into a handstand, and perform strength and hold moves such as the Maltese cross (body parallel to the ground, arms extended laterally), the iron cross (arms parallel to the ground, body perpendicular to mat), and the inverted iron cross. The dismount is a critical part of the routine.

★ UNEVEN BARS: BASIC CONCEPT

Only women perform on the uneven bars. Two parallel bars are set, as the name suggests, to different heights (while height is fixed, gymnasts can adjust the width between the bars to suit their body size). This asymmetric positioning allows gymnasts to jump from bar to bar, demonstrating swings, circles, flips, flying from one bar to the other, handstands, and the always-crucial dismount. Mounts are also part of the scored routine, so gymnasts cannot be assisted on the mount. Instead they must mount either the low or high bar directly or using a springboard.

★ VAULT: BASIC CONCEPT

Both men and women compete in the vault, and for once there's almost no difference between the sexes in terms of skills demonstrated as part of a routine. Routines begin with gymnasts sprinting down a runway and leaping onto a springboard. Depending on the gymnasts' vaulting style, they either catapult hands-first towards the vaulting table, then push off and up while performing twists and aerial turns as part of the landing; or they catapult hands-first towards a mat on the floor in front of the vaulting table, push off the mat and flip backwards onto the vaulting table, then perform some aerial acrobatics. Either way it's a breathtaking display. To score maximum points, landings must be clean with no hops or steps taken.

THE PIXIE PROBLEM

Female gymnasts at the Olympics must be at least sixteen years old, or turn sixteen in the same calendar year. It wasn't always this way: the minimum age for gymnasts was fourteen up until 1981. This led to so-called "pixies"—prepubescent teen-agers— dominating many international competitions (their small and lightweight bodies were simply better at performing acrobatics). The youngest all-around medalist in gymnastics was fourteen-year-old Nadia Comaneci, who won gold for Romania at the 1976 games.

Public pressure forced the sport's governing bodies to raise the minimum age requirements, with some success. The average age of women gymnasts is slowly increasing. The all-around winner at the 2008 games was eighteen years old.

RHYTHMIC

----- DANCING WITH HOOP AND CLUB -----

ONLY WOMEN GYMNASTS PARTICIPATE in rhythmic competitions at the Olympic level (men can and do participate at other levels of the sport). Rhythmic routines feature both individuals and groups of two to six gymnasts performing a range of dance movements (leaps, pirouettes, jumps, and kicks) and acrobatics with sanctioned apparatuses such as ropes, balls, ribbons, hoops, or clubs. Gymnasts can use only one apparatus at a time, and in group competitions only two total apparatuses can be used during a single routine. Each apparatus has its required movements (the ribbon, for example, must remain in constant motion).

Rhythmic gymnastics (individual) made its debut as a full-medal sport in 1984; the rhythmic group competition became a full-medal sport at the 1996 games.

TRAMPOLINE

THE TRAMPOLINE DIDN'T EXIST UNTIL 1936. That's when two gymnasts at the University of Iowa stretched a piece of canvas over a rectangular frame and invented the "rebound tumbler" (initially trademarked as the Trampoline). It became a faddish sport with a massive following, so much so that the first world championships were held in London in 1964—a mere twenty-eight years after the trampoline's invention.

The sport of trampolining made its Olympic debut at the 2000 games with individual events for both men and women. Competitors demonstrate a range of skills (somersaults, bounces, and twists in various positions including tucks, pikes, and straight-body) and achieve heights of 30 feet or more! Routines are scored on overall difficulty, execution, and flight time. The standard trampoline size is 14 feet by 7 feet.

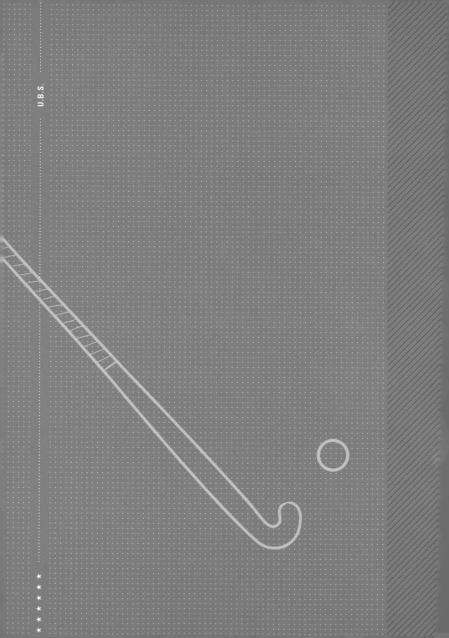

14

Hockey

CHAPTER FOURTEEN

FIELD HOCKEY

----- RUN, STROKE, AND SCORE -----

FIELD HOCKEY IS *NOT* JUST A STRIPPED-DOWN, dumbed-down version of ice hockey. It's a legitimate sport with Olympic credibility (field hockey had its Olympic debut in 1908) and a global base of passionate participants. What it lacks is a fan base. Field hockey is not a popular spectator sport, and no country has a professional league remotely like the NBA, NFL, or NHL. Field hockey could clearly benefit from a marketing makeover.

Field hockey is played by both men and women. Besides the Olympics, the sport's major international competitions are the Hockey World Cup (held every four years), the annual Hockey Champions Trophy, and the Commonwealth Games (only open to countries counted within the British Commonwealth). In international competitions teams from Spain, the Netherlands, Australia, Germany, and New Zealand tend to dominate.

★ **BASIC CONCEPT:**

Two teams of eleven players compete in field hockey to score the most points, by using hockey sticks to pass or push a ball down the field and inside the scoring circle. Once inside, players are allowed to hit, flick, or strike the ball into the opponent's goal. Players must strike the ball with the "face" or flat side of their hockey stick or with the edge of the stick. There are no fixed positions on the field, and even the use of a goalkeeper is optional. Matches are divided into two 35-minute halves and, at the final whistle, the team with the higher score wins.

★ **EQUIPMENT AND PLAYING SPACE:**

The standard hockey stick measures about 3 feet long, with a flat face always on the left side (for right-handed players to make a right-

to-left strike). For safety reasons left-handed sticks are not allowed, ever. Don't even think about it.

Balls are roughly 9 inches in circumference and weigh around 6 ounces (a bit lighter than a standard softball). The field (covered with synthetic turf) measures 60 yards by 100 yards with goals at either end standing 7 feet high by 12 feet wide. A semicircular "scoring circle" is outlined 48 feet from each goal.

★ **RULES AND TERMINOLOGY:**

Most rules in field hockey are designed to keep the players safe. Two umpires monitor official matches and dole out cards to transgressors: green cards indicate an official warning, yellow cards are for a temporary suspension (anywhere from a minimum of 5 minutes and up, at the discretion of the umpires), and red cards indicate a suspension for the remainder of the game. Other important rules:

- » *Up to five players can be substituted, in any combination, an unlimited number of times in a game.*

- » *Players cannot hit or deflect the ball above their shoulders, except when saving a shot at goal.*

- » *Players cannot play or kick the ball with their feet (accidental hits that result in no gain are not penalized).*

- » *Penalties earn the non-offending team free hits (for offenses committed outside the semicircular scoring circles surrounding both teams' goals), penalty corners (for a variety of possible offenses, including offenses that do not prevent a likely goal but are committed in the scoring circles), or penalty strokes (for offenses that do prevent a likely goal committed inside the scoring circles among other offenses).*

- » *Goalies, when utilized, must always wear helmets and protective padding. It's always safety first in field hockey.*

> ▶ |||||||||||||| **VARIANT » INDOOR FIELD HOCKEY** |||||||||||||| ◀

The indoor version of the sport is increasingly popular. It's similar to standard field hockey in nearly every respect except the size of the field (40 meters by 20 meters, with 9-meter shooting circles), and teams are reduced to six players a side.

ICE HOCKEY

----- "SKATE TO WHERE THE PUCK IS GOING TO BE, -----
NOT TO WHERE IT HAS BEEN."
—*WAYNE GRETZKY, ALL-TIME NHL SCORING LEADER*

ICE HOCKEY HAS A LONG HISTORY—a version of the game was played in the Middle Ages in European countries with frosty winter conditions. Yet the real home of hockey is Canada, eh? Gaelic immigrants from Britain and Ireland adapted their traditional stick-and-ball game of hurling to suit Canada's long cold winters. Ice-covered lakes replaced grass-covered fields, pucks replaced balls, ice skates replaced running shoes, and sticks were given a larger curved face for better striking. And thus, a sport was born.

In the early twentieth century professional hockey leagues sprouted up throughout Canada and along the eastern U.S. seaboard. By 1924 the National Hockey League (NHL; www.nhl.com) was firmly established in Canada and the USA as the sport's largest and most important professional association, a position it still holds today alongside the sport's international governing body, the International Ice Hockey Federation (IIHF; www.iihf.com). Hockey has been a full-medal Olympic sport since 1920 and, today, is played professionally in more than twenty-five countries (including the United Arab Emirates and Mongolia!).

★ **BASIC CONCEPT:**

Hockey teams can field a maximum of six players (including a goalie) on the ice. Teams move a hard rubber puck up and down the ice

✶ ✶ ✶ ✶ ✶ ✶ ·········· U.B.S. ·········· ✶ ✶ ✶ ✶ ✶ ✶

ICE HOCKEY

with their hockey sticks and attempt to strike the puck into their opponent's goal or net. Hockey is a full-contact sport, and players are allowed to "body check" (a polite way of saying clobber with a shoulder or hip) opposing players who are in possession of the puck in order to disrupt a pass or shot on goal. Fighting is officially outlawed in hockey, but the game is famous for its gloves-off fights and they are tolerated up to a point by referees.

Professional hockey games are played over three 20-minute periods, and the higher score wins. In regular-season NHL games, tied games add a 5-minute overtime period (teams each field four players on the ice instead of the standard six) and, if the score remains tied, a shootout (three players from each team take penalty shots). In NHL playoffs, tied games are decided with five players in an unlimited number of 20-minute overtime periods, with the first team to score earning the win. At the Olympics, tied playoff games add a 10-minute sudden-death overtime (which, if still tied, goes to a shootout).

★ **EQUIPMENT AND PLAYING SPACE:**

The official size of a North American hockey rink is 200 feet long by 85 feet wide. A red center line divides the rink in half. Two blue lines divide the rink into three zones: a neutral zone in the center, and attacking and defensive zones on either end. The rink's rectangular shape is softened by rounded corners to assist the puck's movement around the back of the goals (which are placed on a goal line 11 feet from the rink's back edge). Hockey goals are 6 feet wide at the mouth and 4 feet high.

Hockey sticks come in a variety of sizes but cannot be longer than 63 inches long. All sticks have an angled blade, used to strike the puck, which cannot be longer than 12 ½ inches. Blades can curve either left or right, depending on the player's handedness. Pucks are made of hardened rubber, measure 3 inches in diameter by 1 inch tall, and weigh about 6 ounces.

Hockey is a fast-moving sport, similar to soccer in its pacing, with few time-outs or interruptions in play. In fact the referees, players, and anything inside the rink are considered "in play" and do not stop play if they come into contact with the puck.

So what does stop play? Icing, offsides, a puck knocked out of bounds or touched by a player's hands, a puck hit with a stick above the shoulders, or when a penalty is whistled by a referee. Icing or "dumping" the puck is when a team hits the puck from their side of the center line beyond the opposing team's goal line (unless the team is on a power play, in which case icing is not penalized). An offensive player is offsides if he crosses the opposing team's blue line ahead of the puck. This is considered just plain rude.

Here are other important rules in hockey:

> » **Checking:** Players can make physical contact with opposing players in possession of the puck, in order to disrupt a play or shot. And the last player who touched the puck is considered "in possession" for up to 2 seconds after passing or losing actual possession of the puck. Checks cannot be made from behind, and it's illegal to use a stick to trip or jab another player.

> » **Goal crease:** Both hockey goals have clearly marked "creases" in front of the goal mouth. This area is off-limits to players with a puck (the point is to give the goalies room to maneuver). Goals scored by players in the crease are disallowed.

> » **Penalties:** Hockey is all about the penalties. Most penalties in hockey result in the offending player or players being sent to the penalty box for 2 to 5 minutes, where they can merely watch as their team skates with one or more fewer players for the penalty's duration. Common minor penalties include tripping, charging (taking more than two strides before making contact with an opposing player), elbowing, high sticking (raising the stick's blade above the shoulders), or holding. A penalty shot is

* **MIRACLE** (2004).

  A gritty, no-frills retelling of the improbable gold medal won by the U.S. hockey team at the 1980 Olympics. Features the unforgettable—and true— line from announcer Al Michaels, "Five seconds left in the game. Do you believe in miracles? Yes!"

* **SLAP SHOT** (1977).

  Not one of Paul Newman's best films. However, it does feature the inimitable Hanson brothers, who are blessed with such lines as "Fuckin' machine took my quarter" and "Hi Ogie, buy you a soda after the game?" Or when a referee warns one of the Hansons during the singing of the national anthem, "I got my eye on the three of you. You pull one thing, you're out of this game. I have any trouble here, I'll suspend ya." To wit, the reply: "I'm listening to the fucking song!"

* **THE MIGHTY DUCKS** (1992).

  Yes, that is Emilio Estevez saying things like "Gordon, stop quacking!" To which Gordon replies, "Quack, quack, quack, quack." Classic.

*awarded when offensive players in possession of the puck are
tripped or interfered with when there are no defensive players
standing between them and the goal. Penalty shots are also
awarded against defending players who attempt to cover the
puck (and thus prevent a goal) while inside the crease.*

VARIANT » STREET HOCKEY

This version of the sport harkens back to ice hockey's distant origins
on the hurling pitches of Ireland and Scotland. Of course, they
didn't have in-line skates back in the day. Nowadays hockey played
by teams of in-line skaters is all the rage, with competitive leagues
across the United States. It's essentially the same game as ice hockey
with a few obvious differences. No ice. No physical contact. And
usually a ball instead of a puck (though some leagues prefer lighter
street-friendly versions of the puck).

15

Motorcycle Racing

CHAPTER FIFTEEN

ROAD RACING

----- "THERE ARE ONLY THREE SPORTS: BULL FIGHTING, -----
MOTOR RACING, AND MOUNTAINEERING.
ALL THE REST ARE MERELY GAMES."
—*ERNEST HEMINGWAY*

ROAD RACING IS ONE OF FOUR MAJOR CATEGORIES of motorcycle sports recognized by racing's international governing body, the Fédération Internationale de Motocyclisme (FIM; www.fim-live.com). As the name suggests, road races are held on purpose-built tracks or closed public roads and there are strict rules about the size of bike that is allowed to compete in each event. All sanctioned road races fall into one of six classes: grand prix, superbike, supersport, superstock, sidecar, or endurance.

Each class has a sanctioned world championship circuit, composed of a half-dozen or more races held on tracks around the world from Laguna Seca (USA) to Doha (Qatar) to Le Mans (France). Riders are ranked on a point system based on their performance at sanctioned race events.

★ GRAND PRIX RACING: BASIC CONCEPT

This is the premier road-racing event, contested on bikes from companies such as Aprilia, Derbi, Suter, Ducati, Suzuki, KTM, and Honda built specifically for racing (all grand prix bikes are illegal to ride on public roads!). Grand prix are divided into three classes: Moto3 (single-cylinder 125cc; "cc" stands for cubic centimeters and is a measurement of engine displacement/power), Moto2 (four-stroke, 600cc), and MotoGP (four-stroke, 1000cc). Racers can reach staggering speeds, up to 217 miles per hour on the fastest MotoGP bikes, which only adds to the sport's spectator appeal.

★ SUPERBIKE RACING: BASIC CONCEPT

What makes superbike racing unique is the bikes themselves: superbikes must be based on production versions of road-legal models. Superbike teams make plenty of modifications, to be sure, but in all cases they must start with a road version produced by sanctioned manufacturers such as Ducati, Honda, and Suzuki. And the final racing version of a bike must maintain the road-legal version's overall appearance. In other words, superbikes must look essentially the same from the front, rear, and sides as their road-legal counterparts. Superbikes can have two different power ratings, 850 to 1200cc for two-cylinder engines or 750 to 1000cc for four-cylinder engines.

★ SUPERSPORT RACING: BASIC CONCEPT

Supersport bikes must be road-legal production models, and the modification options are more strict and limited than modifications made for superbikes. Supersport bikes come in two power ratings,

400 to 600cc for four-cylinder models or 600 to 750cc for two-cylinder models.

★ **SUPERSTOCK RACING: BASIC CONCEPT**

This is another production-model-only category. It's called the 1000cc class because all bikes must have four-stroke engines with displacement capacities no more than 1000cc (two-cylinder models are the only exception and can go up to 1200cc).

★ **SIDECAR RACING: BASIC CONCEPT**

Sidecar racing is thrilling to watch. The sport is exactly what the name implies, motorbikes with sidecars attached and a driver and passenger working together to maximize their speed around the racetrack. In the old days (pre-1970s) the sidecar looked a lot like road-legal sidecars you see on highways today. But you won't find today's racing sidecars at your local Honda dealer. These purpose-built sidecars are slung low and feature aerodynamic fairings to reduce drag. The passenger plays a critical role shifting their weight and leaning into turns to improve overall performance.

★ **ENDURANCE RACING: BASIC CONCEPT**

The point of this sport is to run equipment and teams ragged! Endurance races, as the name implies, run over extended times (anywhere from six to twenty-four hours of literal nonstop racing) to test the durability of motorbikes and the stamina of riders. Teams compete to cover as much distance as possible in a set amount of time. The most famous races are arguably the 24 hour Le Mans and Bol d'Or races in France, and the 8 hour Albacete race in Spain.

MOTOCROSS

----- FOR THE LOVE OF DIRT AND CRAZY-ASS JUMPS -----

MOTOCROSS IS TO MOTORCYCLE RACING what BMX is to bike racing. In both cases roads are replaced with dirt tracks, and highly

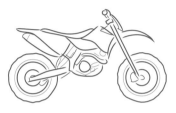

tuned performance bikes are replaced with down-and-dirty machines that can handle seriously rugged terrain. FIM, motorcycle's international governing body, recognizes various categories of motocross sports including freestyle, MX1/MX2/MX3, sidecarcross, supercross, and supermoto.

★ **FREESTYLE MOTOCROSS: BASIC CONCEPT**

Freestyle is the newest sport in the motocross pantheon, introduced as an official sport at the 1999 X Games in San Francisco. Riders are scored by a panel of judges in two categories: "big air" and freestyle. In the latter, riders tackle a course littered with dirt jumps and obstacles and earn points for the skill of their tricks and jumps. One of the most jaw-dropping and point-earning moves is the backflip. Many riders now routinely perform double backflips. Yes, you read right, double backflips on a dirt bike. Seriously crazy. There's talk of banning backflips from the sport, given the increasing number of injuries and even deaths sustained by top-name riders. In the eyes of many, the sport has changed from one showcasing riding skills to one showcasing riding guts and a tolerance for life-threatening risk-taking.

★ MX1/MX2/MX3: BASIC CONCEPT

The Motocross World Championship, the sport's most prestigious circuit, features straight-up racing on dirt tracks (with jumps and obstacles) in three categories: MX1 (up to 250cc for two-stroke engines and 450cc for four-stroke engines), MX2 (up to 125cc for two-stroke engines and 250cc for four-stroke engines), and MX3 (up to 500cc for two-stroke engines and 650cc for four-stroke engines).

★ SIDECARCROSS: BASIC CONCEPT

Yes, some people are crazy enough to ride a rugged dirt course as a passenger in a dirt bike sidecar. Sidecarcross is not well-known in the United States, though it remains popular in northern and eastern Europe. Teams feature a driver and a passenger on a modified dirt bike, with the passenger providing critical weight shifting around turns, leaning entirely out of the sidecar in order to prevent it from flipping.

★ SUPERCROSS: BASIC CONCEPT

This is an exclusively indoor sport for off-road bikes. Given the limited space indoors, supercross tracks have much steeper jumps and tighter turns, making the sport far more technical than the typical outdoor motocross race. The first supercross event was held at the Los Angeles Coliseum, an indoor arena, in 1972. The event wasn't called supercross at the time; but it was such a success with spectators that an entire subcategory of indoor competition was born. It's thrived ever since.

★ SUPERMOTO: BASIC CONCEPT

Supermoto is a hybrid of motocross and traditional motorcycle road racing. Tracks mix dirt and road segments, forcing riders to demonstrate their technical abilities on both surfaces. As with other motocross sports, supermoto got its start in Southern California in the 1970s. Since then the sport has virtually died out in the USA. Instead it has gained a loyal following in Europe, where most of the sport's sanctioned races are held.

ENDURO

----- IN A WORD: ENDURE -----

ENDURO RACES ARE TIME-BASED EVENTS, with riders completing long-distance stages over natural terrain (usually dirt tracks through hilly forests; no more than 30 percent of a course can be on asphalt) in a race against the clock. Yet in a twist, enduro riders don't compete for the fastest times, they compete for the most accurate times. Enduro events give points for riders who reach predefined checkpoints within allotted times. Riders lose points for arriving too early or too late.

Enduro courses range in length from 200 to 2,000 kilometers, usually run in stages to give teams the ability to refuel, rest, and repair. The most famous enduro events are the World Enduro Championship (WEC) circuit and the International Six Days Enduro (ISDE) race. Both feature multiple team competitions for men and women.

TRACK RACING

----- NO BRAKES, NO GEARS, NO FEAR -----

TRACK RACING HAS BEEN AROUND since the early twentieth century. Today three versions of the sport remain popular in the United States: speedway, flat track, and quarter mile.

★ **SPEEDWAY: BASIC CONCEPT**

Speedway is unique in that bikes are not allowed to have any brakes. Riders compete on a flat oval track covered in loose dirt, and use leans and weight shifts to negotiate turns. Typical speedway races feature four to six riders on single-gear (i.e., gearless) bikes. The Speedway World Cup, held annually since 2001, is the preeminent international competition. It's been won five times by teams from Poland, twice each by teams from Australia, Denmark, and Sweden. The best showing by the United States is fifth place.

★ **FLAT TRACK: BASIC CONCEPT**

In the 1950s and '60s flat track racing was the most popular form of motorcycle racing in the United States. It's since fallen on hard times, replaced by supercross and grand prix as the most popular spectator sports in motorcycle racing. The main difference between speedway and flat track racing is brakes: speedway bikes don't have any brakes, flat track bikes have rear brakes. And brakes make all the difference when entering turns at high speeds.

★ QUARTER MILE: BASIC CONCEPT

Drag racing is one of the most popular spectator sports in the USA, and motorcycle racing is no exception. The main event is the quarter-mile time trial, which is a popular benchmark for measuring the speed and performance of a motorcycle. Riders have a mere 1,320 feet to effectively run through the gears in pursuit of the fastest times. Races are held for both superbike and supersport categories, with the fastest times between 9 and 10 seconds at top speeds of up to 140 miles per hour.

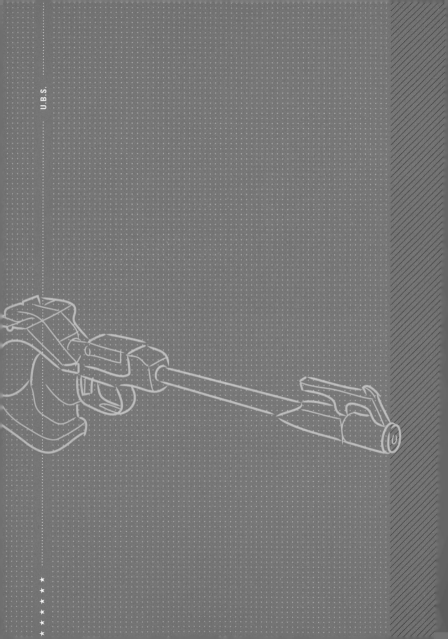

16

>>>

Multi-Discipline Sports

CHAPTER SIXTEEN

>>>

BIATHLON

----- GRAB YOUR SKIS AND RIFLE -----

TECHNICALLY A BIATHLON IS ANY SPORTING EVENT that combines two disciplines. The most famous version is the Olympic biathlon, which combines two seemingly disparate skills: cross-country skiing and rifle shooting. This odd coupling makes better sense in historical context. The original biathlon was developed to train Nordic military officers in charge of patrolling large expanses of snowbound territory.

The modern biathlon consists of a cross-country ski circuit interspersed with shooting rounds split between prone (lying down) and standing shooting positions. Competitors must hit five targets a at of distance 50 meters. Every target missed adds a time penalty to their cumulative time or requires a penalty loop. The goal, of course, is to finish the circuit in the lowest overall time.

The Olympics features five biathlon events for both men and women: individual, sprint, pursuit, mass start, and relay. The individual women's race is 15 kilometers, the men's 20 kilometers. Competitors must hit five targets with five bullets at each of four shooting stops. Every missed target adds one minute to their overall time. The mass start is another individual competition, with up to thirty competitors starting simultaneously on a 15-kilometer (12.5-kilometer for women) circuit with four shooting stops.

In the sprint, competitors stop twice and each time must hit five targets with five bullets (each missed target forces the competitor to take a lap around a 150-meter penalty loop). The top finishers in the sprint are then entered into the pursuit races, where competitors start at staggered intervals. In relay events, each member in a team of four completes a 7.5-kilometer (6-kilometer for women) leg with two shooting stops.

TRIATHLON

----- SWIM, BIKE, RUN -----

THE TRIATHLON IS A RECENT INVENTION. Triathlon can refer to any three-discipline event, but the first official triathlon—combining the now-standard disciplines of swimming, cycling, and running—was held in San Diego, California, in 1974. The triathlon has since become a standard at the Olympics after making its debut at the 2000 Sydney games.

Triathlon segments vary in length, depending on the event. At the Olympics the swimming leg is 1.5 kilometers, the cycle 40 kilometers, the run 10 kilometers. In all cases competitors are striving for the lowest overall times to complete all three events.

A popular variation of the Olympic triathlon is the Ironman triathlon. The only—but crucial!—difference is the brutal distances involved: 3.9 kilometers swimming, 180 kilometers cycling, 42.2 kilometers running (a full marathon).

PENTATHLON

THE ANCIENT GREEKS WERE BIG FANS of the pentathlon, a one-day competition including five skills prized in warfare: javelin throw, discus throw, long jump, running, and wrestling. The competition was revived at the 1906 games, and a modified version was included for the 1912 games, including skills more appropriate for early twentieth-century warriors: fencing, swimming, pistol shooting, equestrian show jumping, and cross-country running.

Today the so-called "modern pentathlon" is a one-day Olympic event featuring those same sports: fencing (sudden-death bouts), a 200-meter freestyle swim, riding a twelve-to-fifteen jump show course,

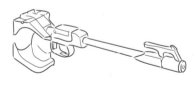

and shooting and running in a combined single event (three shooting segments plus three 1,000-meter running segments). Purists complain the sport should be rebranded a tetrathlon (*tetra* is the Greek word for "four") since running and shooting are combined. Yet perhaps recognizing that *tetrathlon* sounds more like a sci-fi movie than a proper Olympic competition, the name *pentathlon* is staying put.

Either way, pentathletes score points in each of the events, and the score rankings determine the medalists.

HEPTATHLON

THE SEVEN-EVENT HEPTATHLON IS CONTESTED by men and women, but the sexes do not compete against each other and the events vary slightly. The women's heptathlon made its Olympic debut in 1984 with the high jump, long jump, shot put, hurdles (100 meters), 200-meter and 800-meter footraces, and javelin throw. For the men the footraces are run at lengths of 60 and 1,000 meters; the men also pole vault instead of javelin throw, and run 60-meter hurdles. In both cases, heptathletes earn points in each event and the overall highest scores determine winners and medalists.

DECATHLON

----- THE WORLD'S MOST WELL-ROUNDED ATHLETES -----

THE DECATHLON IS THE ULTIMATE EXPRESSION of athleticism. Over the course of two days, decathletes must demonstrate mastery of ten track and field events. The decathlon dates to the beginning of the modern Olympic games, and has grown into a major international competition in its own right. The fact that the Olympic gold medalist is granted the informal title of "World's Greatest Athlete" certainly does not hurt the sport's prestige.

Day one includes the 100-meter race, long jump, shot put, high jump, and 400-meter race. Day two covers the 110-meter hurdles, discus throw, pole vault, javelin throw, and 1,500-meter race. Like nearly all multi-discipline sports, decathletes earn points for their performance in each event, and the overall scores determine the winners.

The decathlon is mainly a men's event, though in recent years there are more women's decathlons at major international athletic competitions.

U.B.S.

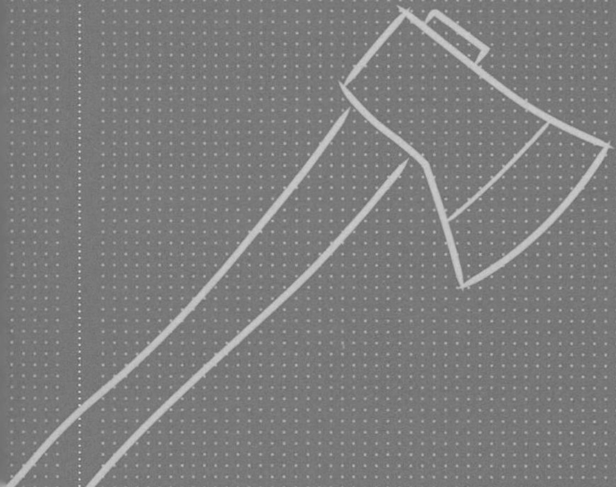

17

>>>

Oddball Sports

CHAPTER SEVENTEEN

>>>

AIR GUITAR

LAUGH ALL YOU WANT, air guitar is an ultra-competitive sport with its own world championships held annually in Finland since 1996. Individual competitors are scored on two one-minute performances, the first to a song of their choosing and the second to a random song selected on the spot. Electric and acoustic air guitars are allowed, as are over-the-top costumes and choreography. Air drumming or air synthesizing result in immediate disqualification, and quite rightly so.

Points are awarded for realism, stage presence, and airness (a subjective category similar to "presentation" in figure skating—i.e., the amount of kick-ass airitude the competitor exudes). In years past winning songs have included AC/DC's "Let There Be Rock," Van Halen's "Hot for Teacher," and "Fell in Love with a Girl" by The White Stripes. The 2011 gold medal was awarded for the first time to a woman (yes, boys, women play air guitar, too).

★ **ODDS OF EVER APPEARING IN THE OLYMPICS**: As a full-medal event, unlikely. As part of the opening or closing ceremonies, definitely!

ARM WRESTLING

----- THEY EVEN MADE A MOVIE ABOUT IT -----

RAISE YOUR HAND IF YOU PAID TO SEE THE 1987 FILM *Over the Top*, starring Sylvester Stallone as a truck driver turned arm wrestler. Nobody? Fair enough.

Despite this cinematic black eye, arm wrestling is a real, popular sport with an international sanctioning body—the World Armwrestling Federation (WAF; www.worldarmwrestlingfederation.com)—and more than forty national governing organizations including the United States Armwrestling Association (USAA; www.usarmwrestling.com).

Professionals stand at a table (they don't sit) and interlock fingers, with elbows bent and touching the table. The object is to pin your opponent's arm onto the table. Matches are divided into classes by handedness (left or right) as well as overall body weight. Rules are strict to prevent injuries. One of the most important rules is that a competitor's shoulder must be in line with, or behind, the competing arm (you can't force your shoulder inwards, as this is a potential way to break an arm).

★ **ODDS OF EVER APPEARING IN THE OLYMPICS**: Surprisingly decent. The sport is highly organized and popular with men and women. Regular matches are held in countries as far-flung as Iran, Switzerland, and the United States.

BATON TWIRLING

----- IT'S NOT JUST FOR LITTLE GIRLS -----

THIS SPORT HAS NOT ONE but *three* international governing bodies! And don't think baton twirling is a mere circus act or activity for kids playing in the backyard. Baton twirling is a physically demanding and highly creative sport, a combination of dance and gymnastics routines set to music with batons twirling nonstop and flying through the air.

The World Baton Twirling Championships have been held annually since 1980 in multiple categories: senior, junior, freestyle, teams, and pairs. The Japanese have dominated world rankings in recent years. Who knew.

★ **ODDS OF EVER APPEARING IN THE OLYMPICS**: Not likely, since rhythmic gymnastics already includes clubs (similar to batons) as a sanctioned apparatus.

NOT A SPORT.
BUT A DAMN FINE COMPETITION.

Ever heard of competitive beard and mustache growing? Better yet—ever seen a photo from the competition? These men take facial hair seriously (yes, it's for men only—women's beard growing would be downright awkward).

The first World Beard and Moustache Championship (www.worldbeardchampionships.com) was held in 1990. Since 1995 the event has become a biannual homage to the lady tickler, trash stash, crumb catcher, soul patch, handlebar, and tea strainer. Competitors are judged in seventeen different categories from "natural mustache" (mustache may be styled but without aids) and Dalí mustache, to Fu Manchu and Full Beard Freestyle. The medal count is heavily skewed to the Germans (think Lederhosen *und* mustache) and Americans (fear the beard).

ODDBALL SPORTS
★ C.17 ★

BOG SNORKELING

THE IDEA IS SIMPLE: cut a trench 60 yards long, 4 feet wide, and 5 feet deep in a peat bog and force competitors wearing flippers, mask, and snorkel to complete two lengths. Standard swimming strokes are not allowed; competitors instead pull themselves along the bottom of the bog or use the doggy paddle. You think we're making this up, but we're not. The World Bog Snorkeling Championship, first held in 1985, takes place annually in August near the village of Llanwrtyd Wells in Wales. The competition is divided into classes for men, women, juniors, and locals. Winning times are under two minutes, and competitors come from as far away as Australia and South Africa.

★ **ODDS OF EVER APPEARING IN THE OLYMPICS**: Ain't never gonna happen.

BOOMERANG WORLD RECORDS

ACCORDING TO Guinness World Records, *the longest boomerang throw ever covered an astonishing 1,401 feet. The world record for longest time aloft is an equally staggering 6 minutes and 20 seconds.*

BOOMERANG THROWING

----- WHAT GOES AROUND, COMES AROUND -----

TRADITIONAL BOOMERANGS ARE LIKE FLYING WINGS THAT, thanks to a unique curved shape, can carve a looping course through the air and return to the point where they were first thrown. The oldest boomerangs date back more than ten thousand years. Despite Australian protests to the contrary, the boomerang was not likely invented by Aborigines—ancient flying sticks have been found in Europe, Africa, and North America, implying that boomerang-like tools were part of the standard arsenal of ancient humans.

Nowadays the sport of competitive boomerang throwing is all the rage in places such as Germany, Switzerland, Japan, Australia, and the United States. The International Federation of Boomerang Associations (IFBA; www.ifba-online.com) organizes a biannual world cup with events for accuracy, endurance (most catches in five minutes), maximum time aloft, distance, and trick catching.

★ **ODDS OF EVER APPEARING IN THE OLYMPICS**: Don't count on it, mate.

CAMEL RACING

----- MORE EXCITING THAN YAK RACING -----

CAMEL RACING IS AS OLD AS HISTORY ITSELF. As long as there have been camels, no doubt, there has been camel racing. And not to pick nits, but we're talking about dromedaries here, not the bactrian breed of camel.

Camel races are big sporting events in India, Saudi Arabia, Egypt, Bahrain, the United Arab Emirates, and Australia (home to the annual Camel Cup in Alice Springs). The length of camel races varies anywhere from short-sprint distances to 10-kilometer endurance runs. Camels are capable of running at speeds of up to 40 miles per hour. Like their horseracing counterparts, camel jockeys guide and motivate their animals during a race.

★ **ODDS OF EVER APPEARING IN THE OLYMPICS**: Get in line behind horse racing, dog racing, pigeon racing, hamster racing, cockroach racing, turtle racing, and yak racing.

CHEERLEADING

CHEERLEADING IS OFTEN A GATEWAY SPORT FOR GYMNASTS and professional dancers. It's also a competitive sport in its own right, featuring choreographed routines that combine dance, tumbling, jumping, and cheering. Cheerleading was once a predominantly American sport, but that's changing thanks to movies such as *Bring It On* and television shows such as *Glee*, which both have large international audiences. The cable sports channel ESPN has further elevated the sport's profile by broadcasting live coverage of major cheerleading competitions in the United States.

The International Cheer Union (ICU; www.cheerunion.org) is the sport's global governing body and sponsor of the annual ICU Cheer Championships. Teams from around the world (USA, Thailand, Japan, China, Germany, Chile, Mexico, and a dozen more) compete in categories such as team cheer jazz, coed premier team, team cheer hip-hop, and coed partner stunt.

★ **ODDS OF EVER APPEARING IN THE OLYMPICS**: Will the International Olympic Committee meet the cast of *Glee*? Then yes, definitely.

CHESSBOXING

THE IDEA HERE IS WONDERFULLY SIMPLE: take the world's top fighting sport and combine it with the world's most competitive strategy game. That's right, boxing meets chess for eleven rounds in the ring. Competitors alternate between 4-minute rounds of speed chess and 3-minute rounds of honest-to-goodness boxing. The first chessboxer to earn checkmate or a knockout wins.

Competitors must be highly ranked chess players (to avoid a situation where Mike Tyson loses round 1 and demolishes his nerdy opponent in round 2). It sounds thoroughly silly, but the sport has a rabid following and is taken seriously by participants. The first women's event was held in 2011. The Bobby Fischer Belt is the sport's highest accolade, awarded by the World Chess Boxing Organization (WCBO; www.wcbo.org).

★ **ODDS OF EVER APPEARING IN THE OLYMPICS**: Absolutely. One has to wonder how this is not the most popular sport on the planet.

COMPETITIVE EATING

----- DOWN THE HATCH AND STAY DOWN -----

IT DOESN'T MATTER WHAT FOOD IS ON OFFER, the goal of competitive eating contests is always the same: eat as much as possible, as fast as possible. It's no coincidence that antacid company Pepto-Bismol is a major sponsor of the sport's proto-governing body, Major League Eating (MLE; www.ifoce.com), a subsidiary of the International Federation of Competitive Eating, Inc.

If you can look past the marketing and aggressive corporate sponsorships, competitive eating is a fascinating sport populated with larger-than-life figures (literally and figuratively) who make it their mission in life to eat more prodigiously than the competition. Arguably the most famous event is the annual Nathan's International Hot Dog Eating Contest, where the goal is to eat as many hot dogs (yes, with bun) in 10 minutes. The record (68 hot dogs) is held by multi-award-winning eater Joey Chestnut (who snatched the record from Japan's Takeru Kobayashi, one of the true international stars in the world of competitive eating). The current multidiscipline record holder, Juliet Lee, consumed seven chicken wings, one pound of nachos, three hot dogs, two personal pizzas, and three Italian ices in 7 minutes, 13 seconds.

★ **ODDS OF EVER APPEARING IN THE OLYMPICS**: Zero.

COMPETITIVE EATING RECORDS FROM MAJOR LEAGUE EATING

- ★ **ASPARAGUS (DEEP-FRIED):** *9 pounds 5 ounces in 10 minutes by Joey Chestnut*

- ★ **BAKED BEANS:** *6 pounds in 1 minute, 48 seconds by Don Lerman*

- ★ **BUTTER:** *7 sticks in 5 minutes by Don Lerman*

- ★ **CHICKEN NUGGETS:** *80 pieces in 5 minutes by Sonya Thomas*

- ★ **CUPCAKES:** *42 in 8 minutes by Tim Janus*

- ★ **DOUGHNUTS:** *49 glazed in 8 minutes by Eric Booker*

- ★ **EGGS:** *65 hard-boiled in 6 minutes, 40 seconds by Sonya Thomas*

- ★ **HAGGIS:** *3 pounds in 8 minutes by Eric Livingston*

- ★ **JALAPENOS:** *118 poppers in 10 minutes by Joey Chestnut*

- ★ **OYSTERS:** *46 dozen in 10 minutes by Sonya Thomas*

- ★ **SUSHI:** *142 nigiri pieces in 6 minutes by Tim Janus*

DEMOLITION DERBY

----- BUCKLE UP -----

DEMOLITION DERBIES OCCUPY THE GRAY ZONE between competitive sport and ridiculous spectacle. There's no denying the sport is a highly competitive, highly dangerous test of driving skills. But really, when all is said and done, drivers are competing for bragging rights and a cold beer—not athletic dominance.

Still, demolition derbies are a constant presence at county fairs and monster truck rallies across the United States and, increasingly, in Europe and Australia. The idea is straightforward: drivers deliberately ram their cars (sometimes trucks, too) at high velocities with the sole goal of disabling the other vehicle. The last driver with an operational vehicle wins the competition. Seatbelts and helmets are mandatory for drivers, thankfully.

★ **ODDS OF EVER APPEARING IN THE OLYMPICS**: Less than zero.

DRUMLINES

THE 2002 FILM *DRUMLINE* GAVE THIS SPORT a brief moment of fame. Drumlines are percussive ensembles, usually part of a larger marching band attached to a college or high school, that compete in categories such as marching drumline, concert percussion ensemble, and soloist. Drumlines have two sections: the battery (marching percussion) and the pit (fixed performers who don't move). Common instruments include snare drums, tenor drums, bass drums, cymbals, xylophones, and chimes, sometimes along with unconventional instruments such as pipes, barrels, and trash cans.

Drumlines are judged on musicality as well as showmanship, choreography, and visual appeal. The largest drumline association in the United States is Winter Guard International (WGI; www.wgi.org), which sponsors local, regional, and national competitions. The sport is also popular in Japan, Korea, Canada, and Germany.

★ **ODDS OF EVER APPEARING IN THE OLYMPICS**: One problem: summer or winter games?

EXTREME IRONING

----- THE THRILL OF ROCK CLIMBING, THE SATISFACTION -----
OF A WELL-PRESSED SHIRT

WHAT STARTED AS A TONGUE-IN-CHEEK STUNT has turned into a proper sporting event combining adventure activities (rock climbing, scuba diving, bungee jumping, parachuting) and ironing. Yes, ironing. Individuals and teams must iron a set of five fabrics while performing their chosen activity. Judges deduct points for creases and burn marks.

★ **ODDS OF EVER APPEARING IN THE OLYMPICS**: Already in. How else do you think the International Olympic Committee irons all those uniforms?

LUMBERJACKING

----- SING ALONG: I'M A LUMBERJACK AND I'M OKAY... -----

LUMBERJACKING IS AN UMBRELLA TERM for sport competitions featuring men—and women—wielding axes. In cultures where

forestry plays an important economic role, there have long been festivals to celebrate the lumberjacks who chop, saw, and fell trees.

The mother of all competitions is the annual Lumberjack World Championships held annually since 1960 in Wisconsin. Gaining in popularity, too, is the STIHL Timbersports Series, which draws men from around the world to demonstrate their traditional logging skills in events such as springboard, stock saw, hot saw, single buck, and underhand chop. The annual Timbersport series is watched by more than 20 million people in 60 countries.

It's fairly amazing to watch a 20-inch log sawed clean in half in less than 5 seconds. Equally impressive are the springboard chopping contests (competitors climb a pole and, suspended in air, chop through a 12-inch log) and logrolling (two competitors stand on a floating log and spin it with their feet, attempting to throw their opponent into the water).

★ **ODDS OF EVER APPEARING IN THE OLYMPICS**: Zero. Deforestation is a tough sell.

MAN VS. HORSE MARATHON

----- LLANWRTYD WELLS DOES IT AGAIN -----

LLANWRTYD WELLS, THE SAME WELSH TOWN that hosts the annual bog snorkeling championships, hosts the equally famous man vs. horse marathon annually in June. The race is run over 22 miles (just shy of an official marathon) and pits around five hundred cross-country runners against forty to fifty riders on horseback. The original idea (fermented in a pub, of course) was to test the assumption that horses are faster than humans over long distances. The first race was run in 1980 and the horse won. It wasn't until 2004 that a human finally did beat a horse.

★ **ODDS OF EVER APPEARING IN THE OLYMPICS:** More likely to appear in the X Games.

SOAPBOX RACING

----- UNPOWERED DOES NOT MEAN SLOW -----

SOAPBOX CARS ALL HAVE ONE THING IN COMMON: NO ENGINE. Which is to say, they all rely on gravity. Soapbox derby racing is a popular and long-standing sport for kids and parents. In the 1990s hipsters in San Francisco and New York gave the sport a second life, holding vaguely illegal soapbox races in urban settings. However, the "official" sport frowns on brakeless cars steered by beer-swilling daredevils. Imagine that.

In the United States, the sport's governing body is the All-American Soap Box Derby (www.aasbd.org), which hosts amateur events across the country including the annual world championships in Ohio.

★ **ODDS OF EVER APPEARING IN THE OLYMPICS**: It's on the list right behind beer pong.

TRACTOR PULLING

----- WHAT'S THE DUTCH WORD FOR REDNECK? -----

TRACTOR PULLING WAS INVENTED BY THE DUTCH, oddly enough. They had the crazy idea to attach a sled to the back of a tractor, toss in some deadweight, and see which tractor could pull the heavy load farthest. The rules have been modified over the years, and now competitors pull the sled over a 320-foot straight track. Sleds are adjusted to be heavier and heavier over the length of the course: A "full pull" occurs on the rare occasion that a tractor reaches the end. Tractors compete in a variety of classes (such as stock, modified, 2-wheel drive, and 4-wheel drive).

The sport has grown in popularity in rural swathes of Europe and the United States. The National Tractor Pullers Association (NTPA; www.ntpapull.com) is the leading organizing body in the United States and organizes annual Grand National Tractor Pull competitions.

★ **ODDS OF EVER APPEARING IN THE OLYMPICS**: *Geen schijn van kans in de hel.* That's Dutch for "not a chance in hell."

WIFE CARRYING

----- COMPETITIVE PIGGYBACK RIDING -----

THE WIFE CARRYING WORLD CHAMPIONSHIPS are hosted each July in the Finnish town of Sonkajärvi. The event started in 1992 as a tongue-in-cheek update of an ancient Finnish legend about brigands breaking into villages to steal local women for wives.

Coed teams of two compete for the fastest time on a 253-meter course over sand and grass and through a water obstacle. Men are not required to carry their actual wife; any woman over age seventeen and weighing at least 49 kilograms will do. Some men prefer the upside-down over-the-back carry, others the piggyback, others still the fireman's hold. Whichever way, it's poor form to drop her.

The event has grown in popularity over the years and now includes proto-qualifying events like the North American Wife Carrying Championship (winners receive money to attend the official event in Finland).

★ **ODDS OF EVER APPEARING IN THE OLYMPICS**: Over Gloria Steinem's dead body.

ZORBING

----- MAKE YOUR HAMSTER JEALOUS -----

ZORBING? IT'S PROBABLY THE MOST DANGEROUS SPORT you've never heard of. Zorbs are double-chamber transparent spheres, anywhere from 8 to 10 feet in diameter. Riders climb in and roll down an inclined slope (not unlike a hamster in an exercise ball). Zorbs come in two varieties, harness or no harness, and can be ridden (if that's the proper term) by up to three riders simultaneously.

The goal of competitive zorbing is to earn the fastest time without deviating from a marked downhill course.

★ **ODDS OF EVER APPEARING IN THE OLYMPICS**: Oddly enough, the zorb has been adopted as the official symbol of the 2014 Winter Olympics in Sochi, Russia. Zorbs made a brief appearance in the closing ceremonies of the 2010 Vancouver Olympics, and clearly they caught the eye of the 2014 Russian organizing committee.

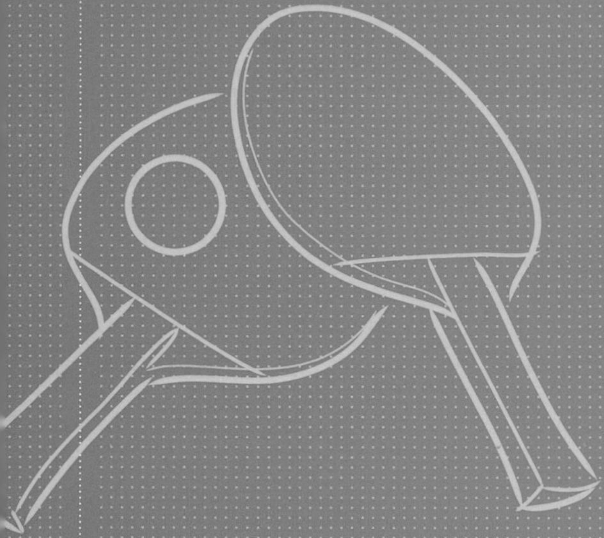

18

Racquet, Paddle, and Stick

CHAPTER EIGHTEEN

BADMINTON

BADMINTON IS NOT A MAINSTREAM SPORT IN THE USA. It's played mostly in high schools and colleges, and after that it disappears from the sporting radar. Which is a shame. Badminton is one of the most physically challenging, fast-moving, and exciting racquet sports around. It's also one of the most popular amateur sports of any type worldwide, with massive followings in Asia.

The game was most likely invented by British officers stationed in India in the early nineteenth century. It was brought back to England and demonstrated in 1873 at Badminton House, and the name stuck. Badminton World Federation (BWF; www.bwfbadminton.org), the game's governing body, was founded in 1934. The sport has been played at the Olympics since 1992.

★ **BASIC CONCEPT**:

Badminton is played head-to-head or in teams of two. Players use a racquet to hit a shuttlecock (a projectile with sixteen feathers tapering to a cone shape) over a net. On the return shot the opposing player must hit the shuttlecock over the net without letting it touch the ground. The rally continues until a player hits into the net or out of bounds, or allows the shuttlecock to be grounded on their side of the net. Games are played to 21 points, and points are earned whether or not the player served. In competition, matches are played to the best of three games.

THE SIXTEEN-FEATHERED PROJECTILE

FEATHERS ON THE SHUTTLECOCK cause it to slow down quickly. Yet that doesn't mean shuttlecocks don't achieve breathtaking speeds on initial impact. The record speed for a badminton shuttlecock hit in a game is a staggering 206 miles per hour.

The court's dimensions are 17 feet by 44 feet (singles) or 20 feet by 44 feet (doubles). The court is divided by a net hanging 5 feet, 1 inch high at the edges and 5 feet high at the middle. Two service lines are marked 6½ feet back from the net. Racquets are smaller and lighter, and have looser strings, than tennis racquets.

★ **RULES AND TERMINOLOGY:**

Games start with one player serving to an opponent positioned diagonally across the court, similar to tennis. Service alternates back and forth: service is from the right when the server's score is even, from the left when odd.

Servers must strike the shuttlecock below the waist and, at the moment of impact, the shaft of the server's racquet must be angled downward (this prevents illegal sidearm serves). The shuttlecock must land on the far side of their opponent's service line or else it's a fault (point and serve go to the opponent). Unlike in tennis, it's okay if the shuttlecock touches the net on a serve as long as it continues over and legally falls in the opponent's half of the service area. If it lands too close, it's a fault.

Other faults include touching the net with the racquet or any part of the body, or slinging or scooping the shuttlecock (it must be firmly hit). If the shuttlecock hits an opposing player, that player loses the point (the theory is, they should have gotten out of the way).

★ **WHERE TO PLAY AND WATCH:**

The BWF sponsors badminton's top competitions: the Thomas Cup for men's doubles, the Uber Cup for women's doubles, and the BWF World Championships (contested by the world's top teams, with China, Indonesia, and Denmark having won the most gold medals).

CRICKET

CRICKET IS A QUINTESSENTIALLY ENGLISH GAME, having first been played in England in the early 1500s. The name *cricket* probably comes from the medieval Dutch word (or Anglo-Saxon or Middle French … cricket has many claims of patrimony) for "stick." Whatever the etymology, the ball-and-stick game known today as cricket was fairly ubiquitous in England as the British Empire was expanding into the four corners of the planet, bringing the game and its unique sporting culture (breaks for tea and sandwiches, matches that last for five days) to India, the West Indies, South Africa, Australia, New Zealand, and more than half a dozen other countries where the game is now played at professional levels.

All of cricket is governed globally by the International Cricket Council (ICC) and the London-based Marylebone Cricket Club (MCC). The game is played in two main versions: test cricket and limited overs. Test cricket strictly means an international match between two of the ten teams recognized as full members of the ICC: England, Australia, New Zealand, South Africa, Zimbabwe, West Indies, India, Pakistan, Bangladesh, and Sri Lanka. Test matches can last for days and often do. Limited overs is a shortened one-day version of the game.

★ ★ ★ ★ ★ ★ ·············· U.B.S. ·············· ★ ★ ★ ★ ★ ★

CRICKET

★ **BASIC CONCEPT:**

Cricket is played by two teams of eleven. One team bats and scores as many runs as possible before each batsman is "dismissed" and replaced by the next batsman in rotation. Immediately behind each batsman is the wicket (two wooden pegs or bails laid atop three wooden stumps), which the bowler (similar to a pitcher in American baseball) attempts to hit. The batsman, on the other hand, protects the wicket and attempts to hit the ball into the field. If the bowler hits the wicket, or if a struck ball is caught by the fielding team before it touches the ground, the batsman is dismissed.

Cricket matches are divided into innings (always plural, unlike the American inning) with one team batting and one team fielding. Bowlers throw in sets of six, with each set known as an over. At the end of each over, a new bowler throws to the opposite batsman. While the same bowler cannot bowl in two successive overs, the same batsman can stay at one end of the pitch and bowl every second over (until they are replaced).

Only two batters are on the field at a time, one at each end of the pitch, playing against all eleven members of the fielding team. Teams switch sides after each innings. The goal is to score more runs than the opposing team and to dismiss the other team's eleven players at bat. Hence the long and unpredictable nature of test cricket matches.

★ **EQUIPMENT AND PLAYING SPACE:**

Cricket grounds are usually oval in shape with a diameter of 140 to 150 meters. The pitch where all the batting action happens is a 20-meter strip in the center of the field, with wickets at either end. Cricket bats are made of wood and cannot be longer than 38 inches, with a striking face no more than 4¼ inches wide. Cricket balls are not unlike American baseballs: hard and dense, covered with stitched leather. Unlike in American baseball, cricket balls are not replaced during the match unless absolutely necessary. The wear-and-tear on the ball is a key part of the bowler's throwing strategy. Also unlike in American baseball, cricket batters wear knee pads and helmets for safety.

Runs are scored when a batsman hits the ball and both batsmen run (bats in hand) as quickly as possible to touch the ground on the opposite end of the pitch behind the "crease" (the safe area for a batsman, similar to a batter's box in baseball) with either their bats or bodies. Both runners must touch for a run to be scored. The batsmen may continue running and scoring until they're at risk of being dismissed. An automatic six runs (no running required) are awarded when a ball is hit over the boundary. Four runs are awarded if the ball touches the ground before rolling over the boundary.

On the defensive side, a bowler delivers the ball to the batter, and the remaining players attempt to catch hit balls before the bounce (batter is dismissed) or hit the wicket while a batter is running (batter is also dismissed). The batsman is also dismissed if his legs block a ball from hitting a wicket (called "leg before wicket"); in cases where the ball is bowled on target at the wicket, the batsman is meant to hit the ball no matter what.

Scoring in cricket is confusing to outsiders. A score of 209/6 means the batting team has scored 209 runs against six wickets (i.e., six of its players have been dismissed).

ENGLAND VS. AUSTRALIA

The first ever test cricket match was played in 1877 between Australia and England (Australia won by 45 runs). It was the start of a rivalry that continues today. When these two teams meet in test play, they compete for the added prestige of playing for the Ashes trophy, awarded in 1882 after the Australians beat England for the first time on English soil, at the Oval cricket ground. A British newspaper at the time ran a story headlined, "In Affectionate Remembrance of English Cricket, Which Died at The Oval on 29th August, 1882…NB: The body will be cremated and the ashes taken to Australia." The English media dubbed the next English tour to Australia as the quest to regain the ashes. The original trophy never leaves its cozy perch at the Marylebone Cricket Club Museum in London (a replica is awarded on the field). And contrary to popular belief, the original trophy does not contain the burnt embers of the wickets played on that momentous August day in 1882.

Limited overs cricket is meant to tame the unwieldy four- and five-day matches that are common in test cricket. The most common format, a one-day match, tries to limit play to a single day by limiting teams to one innings per side (each team bats and fields just once) plus a maximum of fifty overs per side. Twenty20 is an even faster version of one-day cricket: bowlers are restricted to a maximum of four overs, and each side has just 80 minutes to get through their twenty overs.

CROQUET

----- BATTLE OF THE MALLETS -----

CROQUET IS A LAWN GAME, played by striking wooden balls with a mallet through a series of wickets anchored into the grass. It's a lot of fun and a staple of backyard barbecues and family gatherings. The sport also has a competitive side, with international tournaments held in both association and golf croquet. In both games the basic idea is to knock all of a team's assigned balls through the hoops, in proper order.

★ **ASSOCIATION CROQUET: BASIC CONCEPT**

Solo players or two-person teams are assigned either blue and black or red and yellow, and must hit both balls twice through a circuit of six hoops in a predefined order. Once a ball completes the circuit and hits the peg it is "pegged out" and removed from the game.

Players start each turn by striking either of their two balls (players must stick with the same ball throughout a doubles match) at the appropriate hoop. One hoop point plus a "continuation stroke" is earned if the striker's ball is knocked completely through the hoop. If the striker's ball hits another ball (called a "roquet"), the striker earns two extra strokes. The first extra stroke is the so-called "croquet stroke." This is played by picking up the striker's ball and placing it in direct contact with the roqueted ball, then hitting the striker's ball (it has the effect of knocking the opponent's roqueted ball into a poor field position). Strike two is a continuation shot on the striker's own ball.

Besides the hoop point earned for every ball knocked through a hoop, one peg point is earned for every ball knocked into the peg. Points are added together and the winning player or team will end with 26 points (24 hoop points plus 2 peg points).

★ GOLF CROQUET: BASIC CONCEPT

There are two significant differences between association and golf croquet. First, only the first ball through a hoop earns a point and there is no continuation stroke. And second, there are no additional turns for striking an opponent's ball. It's okay (and part of the game's strategy) to knock an opponent's ball off course, but there is no croquet or continuation stroke; play simply continues. As in association croquet, blue and black play against red and yellow. There is no peg in golf croquet. The winner is simply the player or team who scores seven hoop points.

HURLING

----- BOGBALL MEETS STICK FIGHTING -----

BESIDES BEING THE NATIONAL SPORT OF IRELAND, hurling is the oldest stick game still played today (the sport is more than three thousand years old!). Hurling is also considered the world's fastest field sport in terms of game play. Hurling matches are nonstop action, making them incredibly exciting to watch.

Hurling has followed Irish immigrants around the world and is now played at amateur levels in more than a dozen countries including the United States, South Africa, Australia, New Zealand, and Argentina. Ireland remains the only country with a professional league.

★ **BASIC CONCEPT:**

Hurling is played by two teams of fifteen players. Hurling sticks, called hurleys, are used to move the hurling ball, called a sliotar, down the field towards the opponent's goal. Goals are H-shaped and open at the top (like an American football goal) but covered with a net below (like a soccer goal) and guarded by a goalie. One point is scored for hitting the sliotar over the crossbar, three points are scored for knocking it over the goal line and into the net. At the end of two 35-minute halves, the team with the higher score wins.

★ **EQUIPMENT AND PLAYING SPACE:**

Hurling sticks are just that: 40-inch wooden sticks with a slightly rounded end used for striking the sliotar. The sliotar itself is a third smaller than an American baseball and weighs slightly less

(120 grams, compared to a baseball's 145 grams). Hurling pitches are roughly 140 meters long and 90 meters wide.

★ **RULES AND TERMINOLOGY:**

Players can hit the sliotar in the air with their stick, kick it, or strike it along the ground hockey-style. They can also carry it in their hands for four steps, or run down the field with the sliotar bouncing or balancing at the end of their stick. Players can also slap the ball with an open hand for short-range passes.

Hurling is a contact sport, and side-checking is allowed. Players are allowed to use their hurley to disrupt another player's strike or hit, and to hook a player's hurley with their own. Helmets are mandatory, yet no other padding or protective gear is worn. Hurlers are a tough breed.

Fouls are given for minor offenses such picking the sliotar up off the ground (it must be flicked up with a stick or foot or dropping or throwing the hurley). When a foul is called inside the rectangular box surrounding the goal, the attacking team is awarded a penalty shot from the 20-meter line. Only the goalie and two defenders can guard the goal. The penalty is taken by lifting the sliotar off the ground with the hurley and then striking it.

★ **WHERE TO PLAY AND WATCH:**

The Gaelic Athletic Association (GAA; www.gaa.ie) is the sport's governing body in Ireland and organizes hurling's premier event, the All Ireland Hurling Championship. The GAA-sponsored National Hurling League is an annual competition with teams from across Ireland. The GAA is working to bring professional-level matches to other countries. In 2009 the GAA sponsored the United States' first-ever hurling match at the collegiate level (Stanford vs. UC Berkeley).

LACROSSE

LACROSSE IS ONE OF THE FEW MAINSTREAM SPORTS with a Native American pedigree. It was originally not so much a sport as a religious ceremony, with large teams of male warriors competing for the glory of their tribe over multi-day tournaments. Today the sport is mainly played at the college level; the NCAA Men's Lacrosse Championship is one of the NCAA's most popular and well-attended events. A professional league exists, organized by Major League Lacrosse (MLL; www.majorleaguelacrosse.com), with teams in eight cities in Canada and the United States.

Lacrosse is a contact sport and allows body checks and other physical contact. Two versions of lacrosse are played, field and box. Both feature two teams competing to score points by throwing a small rubber ball into a net, using a crosse (lacrosse stick) with a net on one end to capture, carry, pass, and shoot the ball. All players carry crosses, but sizes vary (attackers and midfielders tend to use short sticks, defenders carry longer ones, and goalies use crosses with large heads to help block shots).

★ **FIELD LACROSSE: BASIC CONCEPT**

Teams field ten players at a time in specific positions: one goalie, three defenders who generally stay in the defensive end, three mid-fielders who roam the entire field, and three attackers whose job is to score goals in the offensive end. Attackers and defenders cannot leave their respective zones until the ball crosses the so-called "restraining line" on its own or in possession of a midfielder. Players must also avoid being offsides, which happens whenever a team has more than seven players (counting the goalie) on the defensive end or more than six players on the offensive end of the field.

After a goal, play is restarted using a face-off, with two players laying their sticks next to the ball, horizontally, and competing to gain possession and flick the ball out to their teammates. Fouls are called for violations such as holding and offsides, resulting in a player's suspension for 30 seconds in a penalty box. More serious personal fouls (mainly dangerous physical contact) earn a 60-second suspension.

The standard lacrosse field is 110 yards long by 60 yards wide. Games last for four 15-minute quarters and the team with the higher score wins.

The women's version of the game is hugely popular and plays much like the men's version, though only stick checking is allowed (no body checking or other physical contact).

PROPS TO THE IROQUOIS

THE IROQUOIS NATIONALS, the team representing the six-nation Iroquois League, are the only Native American sports team sanctioned to play internationally. The team has won medals at indoor lacrosse world championships.

★ BOX LACROSSE: BASIC CONCEPT

This is the indoor version of lacrosse. Teams play six-a-side over four 15-minute quarters. The pace is hectic, intentionally so, thanks to a 30-second shot clock and a rule requiring teams to move the ball from their defensive end to their attacking end within 10 seconds. Box lacrosse is the more physical of the two games, allowing a wider range of body checking.

PELOTA

----- ANCIENT TENNIS MEETS HANDBALL -----

PELOTA IS A FAMILY OF SPORTS THAT EVOLVED IN SPAIN AND PORTUGAL in the seventeenth century, loosely based on the French sport of *jeu de paume* (the precursor to modern tennis). Instead of playing face-to-face across a net, pelota sports feature two teams or players standing side by side and striking a ball against a wall or walls. In the various pelota disciplines players use their hand, a racquet, a wooden paddle, or a wooden basket to strike the ball.

★ HAND PELOTA: BASIC CONCEPT

Two teams of one or two players use their hands to knock a hard rubber ball against a two-wall court. The front wall has a narrow playing space; the side wall is much larger. The ball must always hit the front wall and rebound either off the floor or against the side wall. Opposing players can return the ball directly in flight or after the ball bounces once off the floor. Points are scored when the players cannot hit the ball on the rebound, hit the ball out of bounds, fail to hit the front wall on a return, or hit the ball above or below the marked lines on the front wall.

★ PALETA GOMA: BASIC CONCEPT

It's nearly identical to hand pelota, except that players use a wooden paddle called a *paleta* to strike the ball. The ball, too, is different. It's hollow and filled with a gas that enhances its bounce, and thus its speed.

★ JAI ALAI: BASIC CONCEPT

Jai alai, the most famous pelota sport outside of Spain, is popular in Mexico and the United States. Its unique feature is the long woven basket (called a *cesta*) used to catch and throw the ball in one fluid motion. Jai alai balls are dense and capable of reaching extremely high speeds (the official record is 302 kilometers per hour!).

Jai alai courts, called *frontons*, have three walls (front, back, and left) plus the floor. Like in most pelota games there's a dead space on the front wall (in this case the bottom 3 feet are out of bounds). Matches are played round-robin style by individual players or teams of two. The player or team that scores a point remains on the court; the next player or team in line enters the court while the loser(s) go to the back of the line. The match ends when a team scores 7 or 9 total points. The second-highest score earns a "place" and the third-highest score earns a "show." This format is highly conducive to gambling, which is how jai alai was initially popularized in the United States (you can still bet on jai alai at a few remaining frontons in Florida).

RACQUETBALL

----- SQUASH ON SPEED -----

JOE SOBEK IS CREDITED WITH RACQUETBALL'S INVENTION IN THE 1950s. Sobek was a skilled squash player who struggled to find competitive partners. He started playing handball at his local YMCA, but that hurt his hands. Eureka! His insight was to streamline the gameplay of squash, including a more forgiving and easy-to-use racquet, and to combine it with a bouncier ball on a court with no dead zones (the front wall of a squash court has a section that plays out of bounds).

At the time the YMCA had thousands of little-used handball courts begging for a new mission in life. Sobek adapted his game to these courts and starting marketing the sport to YMCAs across the country. By the early 1970s millions of Americans were playing racquetball, all thanks to Joe.

★ **BASIC CONCEPT:**

In racquetball, all surfaces—including the ceiling—are in play. Players compete to score points by hitting the ball out of reach of their opponent. Only the server scores points. Matches are played best-of-three with the first two games played to 15 points, the third to 11 points.

★ **EQUIPMENT AND PLAYING SPACE:**

Courts are 40 feet long, 20 feet wide, and 20 feet tall. A red short line is 20 feet in from the front wall (on a serve, the ball must clear this line) and a service line is 15 feet in (players must serve standing between these lines). Racquets have large heads and short handles, and are strung more loosely than tennis racquets. Official racquetballs are made of rubber, are highly bouncy, and have a diameter of 2¼ inches.

★ RULES AND TERMINOLOGY:

Once the ball is in play, players are allowed one bounce before they must hit the ball (they can also hit the ball before it bounces). On a return hit, the ball can come into contact with any number of walls but must also make contact with the front wall.

Racquetball can be played one on one, two on two, or two on one (players take turns serving to the other players, who form an ad hoc team for the duration of the rally). Other important concepts in racquetball:

> » *Serve: The server bounces the ball once and then hits it off the front wall (hitting any other wall first is a foul, causing the server to lose serve). The ball can touch one side wall, but not two, before hitting the floor, and cannot hit the back wall before hitting the floor. Both of these are faults, forcing the server to a second serve. If the server commits two faults in a row, the serve switches to the opposing player.*

> » *Hinders: If a player obstructs an opponent from reaching a ball, a hinder or penalty hinder is called. The former is when the obstructed player may or may not have returned a rally-winning shot. In this case the rally is dead and service is repeated. In the latter, it's clear a rally-winning shot would have resulted (this is obviously a judgment call and a contentious one at that!). In this case the obstructed player wins the serve or earns a point.*

★ WHERE TO PLAY AND WATCH:

The International Racquetball Federation (IRF; www.international racquetball.com) governs the sport internationally and hosts the biannual World Racquetball Championships. The U.S. Open Racquetball

Championships are an annual grand-slam event for the top men and women from the professional racquetball tours.

VARIANT » PADDLEBALL

Paddleball is like racquetball in many ways. It's played on the same court with most of the same rules. The main differences are the paddles (solid wooden paddles, not stringed racquets), the ball (larger and slower than a racquetball), and the scoring (paddleball games are played to 21 points).

SQUASH

----- WHAT ALL RACQUETBALL PLAYERS ASPIRE TO -----

SQUASH STARTED IN ENGLAND, migrated to the eastern United States, and then grew internationally. Today it's played around the world from Pakistan to Egypt to Australia. It's a fast-moving racquet sport that rewards quick reflexes and aerobic stamina.

★ **BASIC CONCEPT**:

Squash is played on a four-wall court, though portions of all four walls and the front wall are marked out of bounds. Players compete to score points by hitting the ball out of reach of their opponent. A point is earned by the rally winner regardless of who served. Matches are played best-of-five with each game played to 11 points.

★ EQUIPMENT AND PLAYING SPACE:

Squash courts are 32 feet long and 21 feet wide. A red boundary line is drawn on the front wall marked 15 feet above the ground; on the side walls the same line is marked at an angle that drops to 7 feet when it meets the back wall. Racquets have a smaller head than both tennis and racquetball racquets, but are longer than the latter. The rubberized ball is small and hollow, imprinted with color-coded dots that indicate its level of "bounciness." In order from "slow and low bounce" to "fast and high bounce" are orange, double yellow, yellow, green or white, red, and blue. Double yellow is the competition standard.

★ RULES AND TERMINOLOGY:

Once the ball is in play, players are allowed one bounce before they must hit the ball (they can also hit the ball before it bounces). On a return hit, the ball can come into contact with a side or back wall (within the marked boundaries) but must also make contact with the front wall.

In the case of player interference or obstruction, the obstructed player can call for a "let" (the rally is dead and service is repeated) or a "stroke" (the rally is dead and the obstructed player earns a point.

★ WHERE TO PLAY AND WATCH:

The World Squash Federation (WSF; www.worldsquash.org) governs the sport internationally and hosts the World Team Squash Championships, which alternate between men's and women's events each year.

TABLE TENNIS

IF YOU GREW UP IN AMERICA PLAYING PING-PONG IN THE BASEMENT, you probably have no idea that (a) the rest of the world calls this sport table tennis, and (b) professional players can return balls standing more than 15 feet behind their end of the table. Wow. The sport has come a long way since its invention by upper-class Brits in the 1880s. Those early players would undoubtedly be surprised that their leisurely parlor game gained full-medal Olympic status in 1988.

★ **BASIC CONCEPT:**

Table tennis is played one-on-one or by teams of two. Players use small paddles covered with dimpled rubber sheets to knock a small, hollow ball over the net onto their opponent's side of the table. One point is earned by the rally winner regardless of who served, and service alternates every 2 points. Games are played to 11 points.

★ **EQUIPMENT AND PLAYING SPACE:**

Official tables are 9 feet long, 5 feet wide, and 30 inches tall. A 6-inch-tall net divides the table in half, while a white service line (for doubles) divides the table lengthwise. Racquets, or paddles, are wooden with a face 6½ inches tall and 6 inches wide. Racquets can be covered with a variety of surfaces, and even in competition players can use racquets with a spin-promoting surface on one side and a spin-negating surface on the other. The only requirement is that one side is colored red, the other black, to help the opponent see which side is being used on a particular shot.

Until recently the hollow balls used in competition were 38 millimeters in diameter. After the 2000 Olympics a larger 40-millimeter ball was introduced to slow the game down (much to the chagrin of the Chinese, who famously used smash and fast-play techniques).

★ **RULES AND TERMINOLOGY:**

For serves to be legal the server must toss the ball 6 inches straight up, without spin, and hit the ball on the descent. The ball must land once on the server's side of the table and then bounce over the net onto the opponent's side. It's a "let" if the ball touches the net. The server is given one more opportunity to serve before a point is awarded to the opposing player.

It's legal for the ball to come into contact with the hand or fingers holding the racquet, as long as the ball is legally returned. However, players are not allowed to hit the ball twice in succession. A ball is considered fair as long as any part of it touches an edge of the table before falling out of bounds.

Spin is an important part of table tennis. Backspin is where the bottom of the ball rotates away from the hitter, and it's used to slow down the opponent's return shot. Top spin is where the ball rotates toward the hitter, forcing the ball down as it clears the net and then, on the bounce, accelerating the ball's movement—nasty stuff. Corkspin is typically used on service. It's hard to detect and it forces the ball to jump left or right on the bounce. Sidespin, also used on service, forces the ball to hook around on the bounce.

★ **WHERE TO PLAY AND WATCH:**

The International Table Tennis Federation (ITTF; www.ittf.com) governs the sport internationally and hosts the biannual World Table Tennis Championships, which have been won by Chinese players (both men and women) almost exclusively since 1980. The Table Tennis World Cup is held annually and it, too, has been dominated by Chinese individuals and teams.

TENNIS

TENNIS IS THE PREMIER RACQUET SPORT, and the most popular. The sport was invented in the nineteenth century in England, where it's traditionally played on grass surfaces. The rules have changed little since being codified in the 1890s though the pace of the game—and the sheer strength and power of its players—would make the sport virtually unrecognizable to the early tennis pioneers.

Until the 1960s only amateurs could compete in the sport's premier events. Once a player turned pro there were more opportunities to earn money from the sport but fewer well-known events to enter. That all changed in 1968 when the amateur/pro distinction was abandoned, inaugurating the "open era" in tennis when all players could compete in all tournaments.

Tennis's top tournaments, the so-called major Grand Slam tournaments, are Wimbledon (grass), the Australian Open (hard court), the French Open (clay), and the U.S. Open (hard court). In between these events the world's top players compete in dozens of tour and open events, earning points and climbing up the rankings of the Association of Tennis Professionals (ATP), which oversees the men's professional tour, and the Women's Tennis Association (WTA), which was founded by tennis great Billie Jean King and oversees the women's tour.

Tennis is also contested by national teams at events such as the Davis Cup (for men), the Fed Cup (for women), and the Hopman Cup (for mixed teams). Of course, the premier international event is the Olympics, where players compete for both country and individual glory. Tennis was played as a full-medal sport at the Olympics between 1896 and 1924, and from 1988 to the present (it's unlikely that tennis will ever be dropped again, given its ability to draw a global television audience).

★ **BASIC CONCEPT:**

Tennis is played in singles or doubles matches. In both cases players use a racquet to hit a ball over a net, attempting to put the ball out of reach of their opponent(s). Matches are divided into sets and games. It takes two (women) or three (men) sets to win a match, and it takes six games to win a single set. The same player serves for an entire game, and service alternates after each game.

★ **EQUIPMENT AND PLAYING SPACE:**

Official tennis courts are 78 feet long and either 27 feet wide (singles) or 36 feet wide (doubles). The back ends of the court are marked with a baseline bisected by a small center mark. Two service lines are marked 21 feet in from the net. The court is divided equally by a net hung 3 feet high at the center and 3½ feet on either side.

Tennis racquet's hitting area can't exceed 29 inches in length or 12½ inches in width. Besides other obvious restrictions (racquets can't have an internal energy source or be used to communicate with anybody—um, okay!), players are free to use any shape or style of racquet that suits their style of play. Tennis balls are 2.6 inches in

TOP 5 BEST
MEN'S TENNIS MATCHES EVER

★ **BJÖRN BORG VS. JOHN MCENROE**
(1980 WIMBLEDON FINAL).
Borg and McEnroe had a great rivalry, both on the court and in terms of their totally opposite personalities. Borg was the epitome of calm and collected and was a crowd favorite at Wimbledon (the Brits weren't especially fond of McEnroe's mouthy attitude). The fourth set tiebreaker is legendary, lasting 34 points with McEnroe finally winning the game. Yet in the end Borg won the match and trophy, his last time at Wimbledon. Final score: 1-6, 7-5, 6-3, 6-7, 8-6.

★ **IVAN LENDL VS. JOHN MCENROE**
(1984 FRENCH OPEN FINAL).
Lendl was still a relative unknown and McEnroe hadn't lost a match all season. McEnroe took the first two sets easily but then lost his temper at a camera man. McEnroe unraveled and Lendl stormed back to win 3-6, 2-6, 6-4, 7-5, 7-5.

★ **PETE SAMPRAS VS. ANDRE AGASSI**
(2001 U.S. OPEN QUARTERFINALS).
Sampras was at the end of his reign while Agassi
was having a late-career resurgence. After a massive match that included forty-three aces and
twenty-two straight games without a break point,
Sampras clinched it. Final score: 6-7, 7-6, 7-6, 7-6.

★ **ANDY RODDICK VS. YOUNES EL AYNAOUI**
(2003 AUSTRALIAN OPEN QUARTERFINALS).
El Aynaoui wasn't expected to cause Roddick much
trouble. And yet the fifth set of this marathon match
lasted an unbelievable forty games (the Australian
Open doesn't use a tie-breaker on the fifth set).
Final score: 4-6, 7-6, 4-6, 6-4, 21-19.

★ **ROGER FEDERER VS. RAFAEL NADAL**
(2008 WIMBLEDON FINAL).
Five-time Wimbledon champion Federer looked
vulnerable. He was not playing his best tennis
and Nadal took a quick two-set lead. But Federer
stormed back and won the next two sets. The fifth
set was a flat-out gladiator battle with Nadal coming
out on top. Final score: 6-4, 6-4, 6-7, 6-7, 9-7.

diameter, hollow, made of rubber, and covered in felt to give them better grip on a racquet's strings. Balls are also pressurized in their canister to give them more bounce.

★ RULES AND TERMINOLOGY:

Games within a set are won by the first player to win four rallies and thus earn 4 points (and at least 2 points more than their opponent). Tennis has a unique way of scoring these points: love (no points), 15, 30, 40, and game. When two players each have scores of 40 it's called "deuce." The next player to earn a point gets an "advantage" and can take the game by winning the next rally and earning an additional point.

Otherwise, the score drops back to deuce and players are back to fighting for the advantage point. The server's score is always mentioned first, so a score of "40-love" means the server is on 40 and the opponent has yet to score in the game. Similarly, set scores always include the server's score first, so a set score of 4-3 means the server has won four games, the receiver three games. Once a match is complete the winner's score is always listed first (even if they lost an individual set or two).

Other important concepts in tennis:

> » ***Service:*** *Servers must stand behind their own baseline between the center mark and the sideline. Service always begins on the right and then alternates after a point is scored. Receivers can start anywhere on their side of the net but usually stand diagonally opposite the server near their own baseline (to improve their chances of hitting a return). Valid serves must clear the net and land in the opposing player's service box. When a receiver is unable to make contact with a valid serve, it's called an "ace." After the first game, players switch ends of the court switching again at the end of every odd-numbered game.*

» **Let and Fault:** *On the serve, if the ball hits the net but still manages to land in the opponent's appropriate service box, it's called a "let" and the serve is replayed. Servers are not penalized for hitting multiple lets. However, if the service goes out of bounds, is blocked by the net, or hits the net and falls into the wrong service box, it's called a "fault" and the serve is replayed (technically it's called a second serve). Players are allowed just one fault; a second fault gives the point to the receiver.*

» **Foot fault:** *If the server's feet touch the baseline it's called a "foot fault."*

» **Rally:** *Once a ball is in play, players rally by hitting the ball back and forth over the net. Rallies continue until a ball is hit out of bounds or is blocked by the net; or a player hits the ball twice, scoops the ball, or allows the ball to bounce twice on their side of the court. "Volleys" are when a player hits the ball before it bounces on the court, and usually happen when one or both players approach the net during a rally.*

» **Tiebreak:** *If a set becomes tied at 6-6, most major tournaments switch to a game called a tiebreak. A tiebreak is played to 2 points (counted sequentially, unlike in standard tennis games) and a player must win by a 2-point margin. Set tiebreak tallies are often listed in parentheses; for example 7-6 (8-6) means the set score was 7-6 and the tiebreak was won by a score of 8-6. Alternatively tiebreak scores sometimes list only the loser's points, so that 7-6 (6) would mean the loser scored 6 points. Tiebreak are served by the normal player in service rotation. Players switch ends of the court after every 6 points.*

19

Running, Jumping, and Throwing

CHAPTER NINETEEN

CROSS COUNTRY

----- FEW KEEP PACE WITH THE ETHIOPIANS AND KENYANS -----

THIS FORMER OLYMPIC SPORT (1924 was the last year a cross-country medal was awarded at the Olympics) is all about endurance and agility. Runners compete over distances of 3 to 10 kilometers over rugged trails and natural obstacles, often in the rain! Many cross-country events are held on tracks and roads, but the traditional version of the sport is contested on natural terrain.

Official races are run under the auspices of the sport's global governing body, the International Association of Athletics Federations (IAAF; www.iaaf.org). The world's elite cross-country runners compete annually at the IAAF World Cross Country

Championships, which have been won by runners from either Kenya or Ethiopia every year since 2002 (Kenyan and Ethiopian men have won every men's title since 1981)!

ROAD RUNNING

----- 42.195 KILOMETERS IS A LONG, LONG WAY TO RUN -----

AS THE NAME IMPLIES, ROAD RUNNING PITS RUNNERS—often in the thousands—on a predetermined course over public roads. Running's governing body, the IAAF, sanctions races over a handful of distances including 10 kilometers, 15 kilometers, 21.097 kilometers (half-marathon), 42.195 kilometers (full marathon), and 100 kilometers. Races are run by both individuals and teams (usually in a relay format), by both men and women.

Some of the world's most famous road races include the Boston Marathon (considered the original and one of the hardest city marathons, first run in 1897); London Marathon (flat course, great views of the city's main attractions); Berlin Marathon (considered one of the largest marathons anywhere, with more than 40,000 entrants); New York City Marathon (a tough course incorporating all five city boroughs); and the Chicago Marathon. Runners looking for something completely different should consider the Great Wall Marathon in China or the Polar Circle Marathon held in Greenland (brrr!). At the Olympics the marathon is traditionally the last event held, often with a finish inside the Olympic stadium to coincide with the games' closing ceremonies.

How fast do professional runners tackle the marathon? The world record is 2 hours, 3 minutes, and 38 seconds (set at the 2011 Berlin Marathon by Kenya's Patrick Makan Musyoki). A slightly faster race was run at the 2011 Boston Marathon, but unfortunately for Kenya's Geoffrey Mutai, the Boston Marathon is not sanctioned as "record eligible" by the IAAF.

TRACK AND FIELD

----- ALL THE SKILLS PRIZED BY OUR PREHISTORIC ANCESTORS -----

TRACK AND FIELD IS A MULTI-SPORT DISCIPLINE combining track running, jumping, and throwing in a single competition. It's a mainstay of the Olympics and one of the few opportunities to shine a spotlight on low-profile sports such as pole vaulting, long jumping, and shot put. Athletes typically compete as individuals in each discipline, with the best time or distance earning the victory. Many of the following sports also show up in "combined events" such as the decathlon, in which individual athletes are required to compete across all the included events and a single combined winner is crowned.

Besides the Olympics, the most illustrious track and field competition is the annual World Championships in Athletics hosted by the IAAF.

★ SPRINTS: BASIC CONCEPT

Sprints are short-distance races run for the fastest overall times. Distances vary by event, with the most common being 100 meters, 200 meters, and 400 meters. Sprinters start in crouching positions in starting blocks and remain in the same lane throughout the race.

★ MIDDLE DISTANCE: BASIC CONCEPT

The so-called "middle distance" events are the 800-meter and 1,500-meter run (sometimes also the 3,000-meter run). Maintaining a sprint over these distances is not easy, and runners need a fair amount of stamina to outpace the field while still having enough energy in reserve to sprint to the finish line. Runners start from a standing position staggered along a curved starting line, and then head for the inside lane (in 800-meter races runners must stay in their own lane for the first 100 meters).

★ LONG DISTANCE: BASIC CONCEPT

There are two Olympics-sanctioned distances: 5,000-meter and 10,000-meter. Races are similar to middle-distance competitions. No surprise, runners need an even greater dose of stamina and race smarts in order to compete effectively over these longer distances.

★ HURDLES: BASIC CONCEPT

What, running fast isn't difficult enough on its own?? Apparently not, when it comes to hurdles races, which universally feature obstacles about 1 meter high spaced every 9 meters. This forces runners to

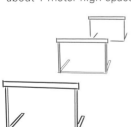

maintain a fast pace even as they jump over hurdles (runners lose time when they knock over a hurdle and can be disqualified for missing one). Hurdle races were part of the ancient Olympics and have featured at every modern Olympic games. Women typically run the 100-meter hurdles, men run the 110-meter and both run the 400-meter hurdles.

★ **STEEPLECHASE: BASIC CONCEPT**

This sport evolved from the equivalent horse racing event. The general idea is for runners to clear hurdle-like barriers (though they don't fall over when hit; runners are allowed to step on and over the steeplechase barriers) as well as a water jump over the course of the race, while still maintaining the fastest overall times. The standard distance for both men and women is 3,000 meters, with each runner tackling twenty-eight barriers in total.

★ **RELAY: BASIC CONCEPT**

This is the only track and field event where teams of runners compete directly (running is typically an individual sport). Teams comprise four runners of the same sex who must pass a baton between them at specified distances, in specified areas of the track. Fumbling the baton inevitably adds additional time to the team's overall event-running time, while dropping the baton leads to disqualification. The most common relay races are the 4 x 100m (four runners per team, each completing a 100-meter race segment) and 4 x 400m (four runners, each completing a 400-meter segment).

★ **LONG JUMP: BASIC CONCEPT**

The running long jump (as opposed to the standing long jump) is a popular Olympic event, combining the excitement of a sprint race with the thrill of watching humans propel themselves as far as possible in the air. The long jump is one of the oldest track and field events with roots all the way back to the ancient Olympic games. Modern competitors are allowed a running start and then launch themselves from a jumping board (their foot must not cross the jumping line). The goal is to jump as far as possible into a sand pit that records the runner's distance (jumps are always scored from the nearest point of sand disturbed by an athlete's body). The current world record jump for men is 8.95 meters.

★ TRIPLE JUMP: BASIC CONCEPT

It's similar to the long jump in that distances are recorded in a sand pit. However, everything else about triple jump is unique. Competitors get a running start and then, from the starting mark, must hop, step, and jump (in three distinct movements) into the sand pit. The longest total distance from the starting mark wins the event.

★ HIGH JUMP: BASIC CONCEPT

The sport is beautifully simple in concept. Competitors must clear a bar that increases in height, in any way they can. There are no fixed rules for how competitors approach the bar, though nowadays almost all athletes use the so-called "Fosbury Flop" method, a backwards-turning head-first movement pioneered by high jump gold medalist Dick Fosbury at the 1968 games. The current world record for men is 2.45 meters in height. For women it's 2.09 meters.

★ POLE VAULTING: BASIC CONCEPT

Here's another wonderfully simply sport concept. Run fast, with a pole, and swing your body over a bar set at an increasing height. Like the high jump, the pole vault has few rules for how athletes approach or clear the bar—all that matters is clearing the bar. Athletes have a running start and then place the top end of their pole in a metal vaulting box, then simply use their momentum to swing up and attempt to clear the bar (turning 180 degrees and releasing the pole as they do so). The pole vault has been an Olympic event since 1896 for men, since 2000 for women. It's an exclusive group of athletes who've cleared a bar set at 6 meters. The current world record is 6.14 meters!

★ DISCUS THROW: BASIC CONCEPT

Think Frisbee with full Olympic trappings. Discus throwing is another event that dates back to the ancient Olympics and not much has changed in the past two thousand years. Athletes throw a 22-centimeter disc weighing 2 kilograms as far as possible, starting from a square throwing area. Discus throwing was one of the very first events added for women at the modern Olympics (starting in 1928). Interestingly, it's one of the few Olympic sports where women outdistance men (the women's world record throw is 76.8 meters, compared to 74.08 meters for men).

★ **SHOT PUT: BASIC CONCEPT**

In the old days (we're talking prehistoric times) throwing a rock accurately was a prized skill. You could argue the skill is a little old-fashioned today. Yet athletes have been competing since the ancient Olympics to throw a "shot" (a heavy round ball weighing 16 pounds for men, 8.8 pounds for women) as far as possible. Athletes start in a 2.1-meter circle and spin to gain momentum. They are allowed to anchor their feet against an elevated barrier at the front of the throwing circle, and then must release the shot from above the shoulders with one hand. The shot must land in the legal area of the field (usually a triangular wedge extending out 35 degrees from the throwing circle).

★ **JAVELIN THROW: BASIC CONCEPT**

Like the shot put, javelin throwing is one of those "comes in handy when hunting woolly mammoths" sports that feels outdated today. That's not to diminish a sport that features men and women hurling a nearly 3-meter-long pointed spear at distances exceeding 95 meters!

★ **HAMMER THROW: BASIC CONCEPT**

Talk about prehistoric! This sport features brawny men and women swinging a hammer (actually a metal ball weighing 7.2 kilograms for men, 4 kilograms for women) at the end of a rope, above their heads, as quickly as possible to gain momentum and then releasing. The farthest throw wins. The Olympics has featured the hammer throw since 1900 (since 2000 for women), and the current world records are 86.7 meters for men, 79.4 meters for women.

RACE WALKING

----- RACE WALKERS GET NO RESPECT -----

WHILE IT'S NOT A RUNNING SPORT PER SE, race walkers achieve a similar body flow as long-distance runners, and must maintain that cadence over incredibly long distances. So don't laugh—race walking is no joke! The sport is contested at the Olympics at distances of 20 kilometers and 50 kilometers. There are only two important rules in the sport. First, a walker's back toe cannot leave the ground before the heel of the front foot is also touching the ground. And second, the weight-bearing leg must remain straight from the point of contact with the ground until the walker's body passes over and through it (this gives race walkers their slightly uncomfortable-looking gait). Both rules are intended to prevent running or jogging strides.

★ ········ **20** ········ ★

Skating

CHAPTER TWENTY

ICE SKATING

----- IT TAKES A SHARP EDGE -----

STRAPPING METAL BLADES TO YOUR SHOES and skating on ice is a common pastime, at least in countries with proper winters. What separates plain old leisure skating from the professional categories is the range of movements and skills involved. Especially in figure skating, the emphasis is on athletic skills presented in highly artistic packages. Both speed skating and figure skating have been full-medal Olympic sports since the first Winter Olympics was held in 1924.

★ **FIGURE SKATING: BASIC CONCEPT**

It's one of the most popular Olympic events, and television audiences for figure skating are always massive. There are three main events at the Olympics: singles, pair skating, and ice dancing. In all formats the focus is on jumps, footwork, and choreography. Skaters are judged on their ability to perform set moves—toe and edge jumps, upright and sitting spins, steps, turns, spirals, and lifts and throw jumps for pairs—and are scored on both technical and artistic merit. Pair skating requires individual skills (skaters are judged individually) as well as aptitude for combined movements. Ice dancing is similar to the standard pair competition, except that skaters are also judged on their ability to perform moves in time to music. At the 2014 Olympics, team figure skating will be presented for the first time.

★ **SPEED SKATING: BASIC CONCEPT**

The Olympics feature two types of speed skating: long track (known simply as "speed skating") and short track.

The former is a head-to-head style of racing for two skaters around a 400-meter-long track, reaching speeds up to 40 miles per hour! The skater who crosses the finish line first wins. Skaters wear armbands to identify which lane they occupy at the race's start (white for inner

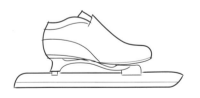

lane, red for outer lane). Halfway through the race skaters must swap sides to ensure they cover an equal distance on the ice. Occasionally this required swap-over results in unintended crashes. Exciting stuff. At the Olympics

races are skated at distances of 500 meters, 1,000 meters, 1,500 meters, 5,000 meters, and 10,000 meters. There are also team pursuit events, which pit two teams of three skaters in direct competition (instead of against the clock) starting from opposite sides of the rink. If one team overtakes the other, it automatically wins the race.

Short track is a "mass start" event with multiple skaters, as opposed to the head-to-head format in long track racing. Short track races are held on hockey rinks, which are typically 111 meters in circumference. Events are held for both men and women at distances of 500 meters, 1,000 meters, 1,500 meters, and 3,000 metters. There are also team relay events at distances of 3,000 meters (women) and 5,000 meters (men).

IN-LINE SKATING

----- STRAIGHT-UP ARTISTRY -----

IN-LINE SKATES WERE ALL THE RAGE IN THE 1990S, as traditional quad skates (the four-wheel roller skates your parents grew up with) gave way to mono skates with a single line of wheels. In-line skates are faster and more maneuverable than traditional roller skates, and mimic speed skating on ice (so much so, in fact, that professional speed skaters often race in-line skates during the off-season).

★ IN-LINE SPEED SKATING: BASIC CONCEPT

In-line speed skating has evolved far beyond ad hoc competitions at the local park. The sport features sprints, time trials, elimination races, and relays organized on oval-shaped tracks not unlike velodromes. The sport's two governing bodies—the National Inline Racing Association (NIRA; www.sk8nira.com) and the International Roller Sports Federation (FIRS; www.rollersports.org)—are lobbying for inclusion at the summer Olympics, so far to no avail. Until then the sport's premier competition is the annual World Roller Speed Skating Championships.

★ **IN-LINE DOWNHILL SKATING: BASIC CONCEPT**

It's a lot like it sounds, racing against a field of competitors for the best time on a downhill course, at breakneck speeds. Competitors wear helmets and padding, and only in-line skates are allowed at official sanctioned events including the annual Inline Downhill World Championships.

★ **IN-LINE FREESTYLE SKATING: BASIC CONCEPT**

Freestyle comes in several categories, including classic freestyle, freestyle battle, and speed slalom. In freestyle slalom, individual skaters perform choreographed routines to music, and get 90 seconds to show off their tricks to the judges. Skaters compete for points, and the highest score wins. In freestyle battle, groups of four skaters each get 30 seconds to dazzle judges on a short slalom course. The top two skaters advance to the next round. In the speed slalom, two skaters compete head-to-head on a course with twenty cones. The fastest time, with penalty time added for touched or missed cones, wins.

ROLLER SKATING

----- QUAD SKATING AIN'T DEAD -----

THE RUMORS OF QUAD SKATING'S DEMISE are greatly exaggerated. While it's true that in-line skating has skyrocketed in popularity over the past twenty years, traditional quad skating is going strong as both a leisure activity and a competitive sport.

★ ARTISTIC SKATING: BASIC CONCEPT

Artistic roller skating is heavily influenced by figure ice skating, with its own set of disciplines (figures, freestyle, pairs, dance, precision) performed exclusively on quad skates in competition. One of the main differences between the ice and non-ice versions is the use of markings on the rink. In the figures discipline of artistic roller skating, skaters trace circles painted on the skating surface and are judged on their ability to follow the patterns without skating outside the lines.

★ RINK HOCKEY: BASIC CONCEPT

Rink hockey is another competitive quad-skate sport, played on a rectangular ice-hockey-like rink between two teams of five players each (including goalkeepers). As in hockey, players use sticks to knock a ball (instead of a puck) into a net to score points.

★ ROLLER DERBY: BASIC CONCEPT

Roller derby is a full-on contact sport, often played by all-women teams (though coed and men teams are not unheard of). Two teams of five skate in the same direction around an oval flat rink. The goal is for a single scoring player (called the "jammer") to outlap the opposing team (after making it through the pack of blockers once, the jammer scores points for each opposing blocker she passes legally and in bounds). Everybody else on the rink tries to hinder the opposing jammer with blocks (it's legal to body check opponents between the shoulders and mid-thigh; elbowing or tripping earns players a minute in the penalty box) while clearing a path for their own jammer.

For many years roller derby was more entertainment than sport, not unlike professional wrestling in the USA, which was and is highly scripted (more theatrical performance than athletic competition). But roller derby has undergone a rebirth in the past decade, with serious amateur leagues sprouting up across the USA and internationally. In the United States the sport is governed by the Women's Flat Track Derby Association (WFTDA; www.wftda.com).

TOP 5 ROLLER DERBY TEAM NAMES

★ **AULD REEKIE ROLLER GIRLS** (EDINBURGH, SCOTLAND)

★ **BREWCITY BRUISERS** (MILWAUKEE, WISCONSIN)

★ **DOCKYARD DERBY DAMES** (TACOMA, WASHINGTON)

★ **HARD KNOX ROLLER GIRLS** (KNOXVILLE, TENNESSEE)

★ **SLAUGHTER COUNTRY ROLLER VIXENS**
(KITSAP COUNTY, WASHINGTON)

SKATEBOARDING

----- IT'S WHAT YOU DO IN AN EMPTY SWIMMING POOL -----

THERE'S NO DENYING IT, skateboarding gets little respect in the world of competitive sports. Blame its bad-boy, pot-smoking, punk-thrasher image, a holdover from skateboarding's early days as a counter-culture movement born in Southern California in the 1970s. Whatever the reason, skateboarding's overwhelming popularity has continually struggled to translate into mainstream success as an amateur or professional sport.

Recently the Street League Skateboarding organization has tried to create a professional street skateboarding series. The sport's semiofficial governing body, World Cup Skateboarding (WCS; www.wcsk8.com), also sponsors professional competitions each year in categories including vertical, bowl, and street events such as the Dew Tour and X Games, both of which draw large global television audiences. Along with global audiences come major sponsors with money to spend on prize money, which also helps the sport attract a cadre of hardcore amateurs and pros.

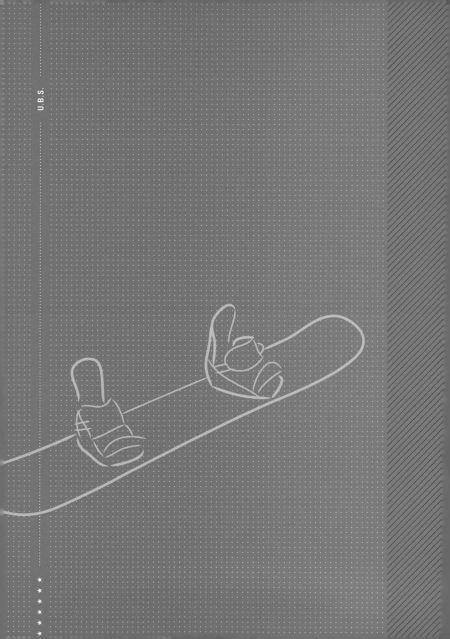

21

Ski and Snow

CHAPTER TWENTY-ONE

ALPINE SKIING

----- GOING DOWNHILL FAST -----

ALPINE SKIING REFERS TO MOST ANY ACTIVITY on skis using fixed-heel bindings. The binding—and the changes in gear and skiing style that come with a fixed-heel binding—are what distinguish it from other ski styles such as cross-country and Telemark.

In the competitive sphere, alpine skiing is divided into four categories at premier events such as the Winter Olympics: slalom (SL), giant slalom (GS), super-giant slalom (Super-G), and downhill (DH). All major ski competitions are held under the auspices of the sport's governing body, the International Ski Federation (FIS; www.fis-ski.com).

★ SLALOM: BASIC CONCEPT

All slalom races involve skiing at high speeds between poles, or gates, placed about 30 vertical feet apart and offset horizontally about 7 feet. This tight spacing and narrow offset means slalom racing demands tighter, quicker turns, which makes the sport highly technical and probably the most physically demanding of any alpine ski discipline. The typical slalom course has sixty to seventy-five gates (men) or forty-five to sixty gates (women). Racers run the course twice for a combined total time.

★ GIANT SLALOM: BASIC CONCEPT

By "giant" they really just mean "gates spaced farther apart" compared to standard slalom. That's the main difference between these two disciplines.

★ SUPER-GIANT SLALOM: BASIC CONCEPT

Unlike the more technical slalom and giant slalom racing styles, super-giant slalom is more about speed and less about quantity of tight turns. Super-G races have fewer gates spaced farther apart, and often are run on steeper slopes to generate more downhill momentum.

★ DOWNHILL: BASIC CONCEPT

This is the fastest and most dangerous alpine style. Downhill racers can exceed 75 or 80 miles per hour as they negotiate jumps and turns in the most aerodynamic positions possible. Every bit of drag must be reduced, as the margin separating elite downhill racers can be fractions of seconds. Skiers do a single run (as opposed to combined runs) and the lowest time wins.

★ FREESTYLE: BASIC CONCEPT

Freestyle alpine skiing attempts to capture some of the coolness factor associated with snowboarding. Alpine freestyle events include everything from moguls to jumps and aerials.

This is a sport for daredevils on skis. Ski jumpers launch themselves down a takeoff ramp and fly as far as possible before landing. Points are scored for both style and distance achieved. Jumpers use skis that are longer and wider than standard recreational skis, to give them more stability on the ramp and more aerodynamic balance in the air. Jump distances of 350 to 425 feet are common. At the Olympics each jumper goes twice and the scores are combined.

CROSS-COUNTRY SKIING

----- THE ULTIMATE DIET, GUARANTEED TO BURN CALORIES -----
LIKE NO OTHER SPORT CAN

HUNTING IS THE HISTORICAL GENESIS OF CROSS-COUNTRY SKIING. In ancient times, hunters on primitive skis would track animals over the flat terrain of northern Europe. Cross-country skiing still favors flat or gently hilly terrain to the steep downhill slopes of alpine skiing. Because of this change of emphasis, cross-country skis themselves are a different beat altogether: skis are longer and narrower than alpine skis (to better distribute a skier's weight) and have heelless bindings to allow greater mobility of the foot. Either way, cross-country skiing is considered among the most physically demanding and calorie-burning sports.

Skis come in two general styles, those for classic tramping through snow, or combination skis tailored for tramping as well as for a skating-style of movement that produces greater speeds. Cross-country competition features sprints, relays, and pursuits, both individual and team, over distances ranging from 10 to 50 kilometers. Cross-country is also featured in sports such as the biathlon (shooting and skiing).

COMPETITIVE SLEDDING

----- HALF-PIPE ON ICE -----

SLEDS HAVE EXISTED FOR CENTURIES. Yet all three modern sledding sports—skeleton (head first), luge (feet first), and bobsled (sitting)—were pioneered in the 1870s on the world's first purpose-built, half-pipe sledding course at St. Moritz, Switzerland. The bobsled made its debut at the first Winter Olympics in 1924; skeleton followed in 1928, luge in 1964. All three sports are now regularly contested at the Olympics. International competitions are governed by the International Bobsleigh & Skeleton Federation (FIBT; www.fibt.com).

★ BOBSLED: BASIC CONCEPT

Bobsleds are two- or four-person covered sleds powered only by gravity. Sleds achieve maximum speeds of 80 to 90 miles per hour. Racers shift their own weight to help navigate turns, and the lead racer pilots the sled with gentle pulls on cables attached to the bobsled's steel blades (though realistically there's little steering required in bobsled, since the sleds tend to follow grooves in the ice). After crossing the finish line it's the brakeman's job to slow the bobsled. At the Olympics women compete in two-woman bobsled, men in two- and four-man bobsled. Races begin from a standing start.

★ **LUGE: BASIC CONCEPT**

The luge is a small uncovered sled intended for one or two racers who ride feet-first on their backs. Unlike the bobsled, luges are highly navigable. Racers need to select the best line possible through the turns and use their legs to flex the sled's steel runners in one direction or the other. Racers can also use their shoulders to induce a turn. Luges reach speeds of 85 to 90 miles per hour.

★ **SKELETON: BASIC CONCEPT**

The skeleton is a one-person sled that racers operate head-first and lying down. Like the luge, the skeleton is highly maneuverable and achieves speeds of up to 85 miles per hour. Skeletons use the same tracks as bobsleds and luges.

DOGSLED RACING

----- MUSH! -----

THE WORLD OF COMPETITIVE DOGSLED RACING IS A SMALL but fascinating one. Competitors and their much-loved animals often battle extreme conditions in remote locations, which clearly is part of the sport's appeal. Races are run at a variety of lengths (anywhere from 5 to 200 miles, sometimes longer) yet races are categorized not by distance, but by the maximum number of dogs with which each team is allowed to travel. Common categories include four-dog, six-dog, and eight-dog. Open races allow an unlimited number of canine competitors. Sled dogs wear individual harnesses connected to tuglines, which in turn are connected to a central gangline controlled by the sled driver.

Hands-down the most famous dogsled race is the annual 1,049-mile Iditarod, which pits teams of up to sixteen dogs racing for the fastest time between Anchorage and Nome, Alaska.

Dogsledding was a demonstration sport at the 1932 and 1952 Winter Olympics. It's unlikely to make an Olympic return anytime soon.

SNOWBOARDING

----- FREESTYLIN' -----

SNOWBOARDING HAS STRUGGLED HARD to shed its "bad boy" attitude. For many years, especially in the 1970s and early '80s when the sport was still new, snowboarding was an outcast at ski resorts and

relegated to third-tier competitions organized by diehard fans with limited sponsorships. That started to change in 1985 with the first Snowboarding World Cup. The sport gained the ultimate imprimatur of respectability when four snowboarding events were included as full-medal competitions at the 1998 Winter Olympics.

Snowboarding events at the Olympics include half-pipe (boarding a large half-pipe course with an emphasis on tricks, jumps, and aerial maneuvers), parallel giant slalom (head-to-head racing on a standard slalom course) and snowboard cross (head-to-head racing on a course with obstacles and jumps).

★ ···· **22** ···· ★

>>

Soccer
CHAPTER TWENTY-TWO

>>

ASSOCIATION FOOTBALL

IN THE SPIRIT OF CALLING A SPADE A SPADE, this chapter is titled "soccer." And yet the sport under the spotlight is called association football.

What's up with that?

The original name of the sport most Americans call soccer is association football. The rules of the sport were first codified in the 1860s by the Football Association (FA; www.thefa.com) in England, and the name stuck. Even at the international level, the sport's global governing body is the Fédération Internationale de Football Association (FIFA; www.fifa.com). Clearly the name "association football" has a long and glorious history.

U.B.S.

ASSOCIATION FOOTBALL

Oddly enough, the word "soccer" was itself coined from the name *association football*. Take the word *association* and abbreviate it. That's how the word "assoc." evolved into the word "soccer" in England. For most of the twentieth century the game was known interchangeably as either soccer or football.

However, especially in the United States, nowadays the sport is called soccer almost exclusively (acknowledging this fact, the sport's American governing body changed its name in the 1970s from U.S. Football Association to U.S. Soccer). Is there a flipside to this coin? Of course there is. Muddying the already murky waters are Major League Soccer clubs such as FC Dallas, Seattle Sounders FC, and Vancouver Whitecaps FC (all of which add the abbreviation "Football Club," or FC, to their names). The bottom line: you can legitimately call it soccer of football, just don't call it soccer football.

Soccer is universally considered the world's most popular spectator sport. Major tournaments such as the FIFA World Cup, FIFA Women's World Cup, and the summer Olympics (soccer has been a medal sport since 1990) draw television audiences measured in billions with a "b." National leagues such as England's Premier League, Germany's Bundesliga, Italy's Serie A, France's League 1, and Brazil's Football League draw major national and international audiences. Even Major League Soccer (MLS; www.mlssoccer.com) is having success attracting sports-saturated Americans to professional soccer, with nineteen teams playing in the USA and Canada.

★ **BASIC CONCEPT:**

Two teams of eleven players (including goalkeepers) attempt to score goals by moving the soccer ball down the field and into the opponent's goal. All players (except goalkeepers) cannot touch the ball with their hands or arms; players instead kick the ball with their feet or redirect a moving ball with their heads.

Soccer is a fast-moving game, with numerous changes of possession. Soccer matches are divided into 45-minute halves and the game clock is only stopped when the ball is out of bounds or when a penalty is called by a referee. At the end of roughly 90 minutes (a few extra minutes are often added to the game clock by the referee for injury time) the team with the higher score wins. Ties end in draws (except at major tournaments, when the game goes into extra time and/or a penalty shootout, depending on the format of the competition).

★ **EQUIPMENT AND PLAYING SPACE**

Soccer fields are called "pitches" and there is no single rule or law for defining a pitch's size. The international standard is 100 to 110 meters

in length, 65 to 75 meters in width. The long boundaries on a pitch are called touch lines, the short boundaries are called goal lines. Two goals measuring 7.3 meters across and 2.44 meters tall stand at opposite ends of the pitch, centered on each goal line. Both goals are surrounded by a penalty area extending 16.5 meters into the pitch. This establishes the maximum point at which goalies can handle the ball with their hands.

The ball itself is a sphere with a circumference of 71 centimeters and a weight of 450 grams (aka size 5 on the international scale of soccer balls).

★ **RULES AND TERMINOLOGY:**

There are no official positions in soccer except goalkeeper. Some players do specialize in certain tasks, and teams on the field are unofficially organized into "strikers" (forward-positioned players focused on scoring goals), midfielders (focused on dispossessing opposing players and feeding balls to their strikers), and defenders (focused on preventing opposing players from scoring).

TOP 10 MEN'S SOCCER PLAYERS

★ **PELÉ** (PLAYED 1956–77).
   At the tender age of seventeen, Pelé scored six
   goals at the 1958 World Cup, leading Brazil to its
   first title.

★ **DIEGO MARADONA** (PLAYED 1976–97).
   Love him or hate him, Maradona is unquestionably
   Argentina's best player, ever. You just need to look
   past the drug allegations and the "hand of God"
   goal he scored illegally in the 1986 World Cup
   quarter-final match against England.

★ **FRANZ BECKENBAUER** (PLAYED 1964–83).
   He's the only player to both captain and manage
   teams that won a World Cup (1974 and 1990,
   respectively). As a player he led his team Bayern
   Munich to three European Cup championships
   and four national titles.

★ **ZINEDINE ZIDANE** (PLAYED 1988–06).
Zidane led France to victory at the 1998 World Cup and Euro 2000, in addition to helping his team Real Madrid win the 2002 UEFA Champions League. He is one of just three three-time FIFA World Player of the Year winners.

★ **LEV YASHIN** (PLAYED 1951–70).
He's the only goalkeeper on the list, playing for Dynamo Moscow in the Soviet Top League and saving a miraculous 150 penalty shots over his career. He's one of only two Soviet players ever named European Footballer of the Year.

★ **BOBBY CHARLTON** (PLAYED 1956–76).
He scored 49 international goals for England and played for seventeen seasons with Manchester United, helping the club to win its first European Cup.

★ **JOHAN CRUYFF** (PLAYED 1964–84).
This Dutch player and manager/coach was named European Footballer of the Year three times. He came in second (behind Pelé) in the 1999 World Player of the Century poll.

★ **RONALDO LUIS NÁZARIO DE LIMA**
(PLAYED 1993–2011).
Ronaldo played on Brazil's World Cup teams in
1998 (Brazil lost 0–3 to France in the finals), 2002
(Brazil won the tournament, beating Germany 2–0
in the finals), and 2006 (Brazil was eliminated in
the quarter finals).

★ **GERD MÜLLER** (PLAYED 1963–81).
Germany's Müller scored 68 goals in 62 international appearances, 365 goals in 427 Bundesliga
games, and 66 goals in 74 European Club games.
He currently ranks eighth on the list of all-time
international goal scorers.

★ **MICHEL PLATINI** (PLAYED 1972–87).
He was the leading scorer when France won the
1984 European Championship. He is considered
one the best passers in football history.

Soccer is a limited-contact sport. Players can use their legs and feet to legally tackle an opposing player in possession of the ball; however, the target must always be the ball (not the opposing player's feet or legs). Tackling with both legs or from behind is illegal.

Other important rules in soccer include:

» **Handball:** *Only goalkeepers can play the ball with their hands or arms, as long as they are inside their own penalty area. Otherwise a handball penalty is called by the referee.*

» **Goal kick:** *A goal kick is awarded when a ball crosses the goal line and was last touched by an opposing player. The ball is placed anywhere in the defending goal area and must be kicked (goalkeepers are not allowed to pick up the ball).*

» **Free kick:** *There are two types of free kick, indirect and direct. The former are awarded for minor fouls and cannot score without first touching another player. Direct free kicks are awarded for serious penalties and can score without first being touched by other players.*

» **Corner kick:** *Awarded when a ball crosses the goal line and was last touched by a defending player (including the goalie). The opposing team places the ball in the corner closest to where the ball crossed the goal line and is allowed a direct-kick attempt into the goal.*

» **Penalty kick:** *Awarded for serious fouls inside the penalty box. The opposing team positions the ball on a penalty mark 11 meters from the goal. The penalty kicker (who does not have to be the same player who was fouled) is allowed a direct free kick attempt on goal.*

» **Offside:** *Attacking players are offside when they are in the opponent's half of the pitch and closer to the opponent's goal line than both the ball and the second-to-last defender (the goalkeeper is usually the "last defender"). A player won't be* called offside if they do not actively participate in the current play.

» **Penalties:** Referees award minor penalties for illegal tackles and improper contact. Major penalties are awarded for dangerous tackles, intentional tripping, and serious breaches of sportsmanship and are accompanied by a yellow card (caution) or red card (immediate suspension). Players shown a yellow card are "booked" and the referee writes their name in an official notebook. A second yellow card in the same game leads to an automatic red card. When players are suspended, substitute players cannot be brought on to replace them.

» **Substitutions:** Up to three players can be substituted in international competitions. When players are substituted off the field they cannot play for the remainder of the game, including extra time or penalty shootouts.

GAELIC FOOTBALL

----- SCORE THE IRISH THREE POINTS FOR CREATIVITY -----

IRELAND'S SECOND MOST FAVORITE GAME (after hurling) is Gaelic football. It shares many traits with association football, with a heavy dose of hurling, Australian Rules football, and rugby thrown in for good measure. At first glance Gaelic football seems absolutely chaotic: the game is played with both hands and feet, and the player holding the ball is only allowed to take four steps before tossing the ball to the ground and kicking it to a teammate. Crazy stuff.

★ BASIC CONCEPT:

Two teams of fifteen compete to score points with a round soccer-like ball. Unlike standard soccer goals, Gaelic football goals are H-shaped. Players can kick the ball over the crossbar (or punch it over with their fist) for 1 point. Kicking the ball *below* the crossbar is considered a goal and scores 3 points.

The other key difference is that players are allowed to pass the ball with their hands with a closed-fist punch (similar to Australian Rules football). Players cannot pick up the ball directly from the ground, though they can kick or scoop it into their hands using their feet. Players cannot move more than four steps without kicking, bouncing, or "soloing" the ball (kicking the ball from one's feet to hands). As you may have guessed, Gaelic football is way more physical than standard soccer, with more tolerance for tackles and shoulder-to-shoulder contact.

In Ireland, Gaelic football is supervised by the Gaelic Athletic Association (GAA; www.gaa.ie). Dublin's Croke Park stadium hosts the annual All-Ireland Gaelic Football Finals.

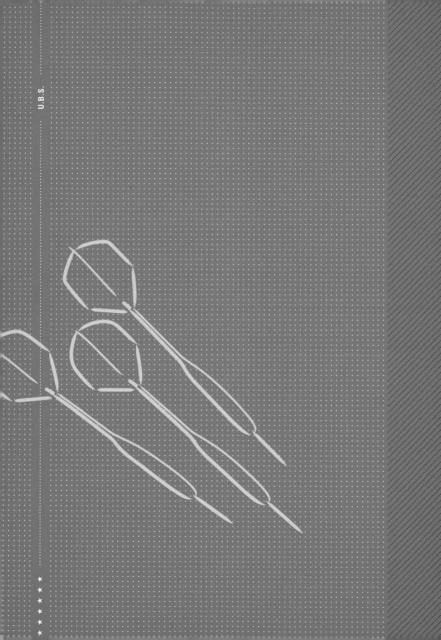

Target Sports

CHAPTER TWENTY-THREE

ARCHERY

----- AIM FOR THE GOLDEN RING -----

THE BOW AND ARROW IS AN ANCIENT TOOL. Primitive humans strung a dried animal intestine between notches in branches or animal horns, and fired pointed shafts carved from wood or bone. These basic setups, along with the more powerful longbows and crossbows, were used for hunting and as weapons well into the seventeenth century. Hunting bows are still in use, though the sport of archery is now more about accuracy at a distance than about hunting down prey.

Archery was contested at the early modern Olympic games, fell out of favor for a few decades, and was reintroduced as a full-medal sport at the 1972 Olympics. There are individual and team competitions for both men and women, usually taking the form of shooting sets of three arrows at a target from 70 meters. Targets have ten concentric rings, with inner (and smaller) circles scoring more points than outer rings. The countries to beat at the Olympics are the South Koreans and Americans—men and women from both nations dominate the competition.

DARTS

DARTS IS A BROAD CATEGORY, encompassing everything from challenge matches at your local pub or bar to professional matches sanctioned by the sport's two governing bodies, the World Darts Federation (WDF; www.dartswdf.com) and the Professional Darts Corporation (PDC; www.pdc.tv).

In professional darts the idea is simple: two competitors take turns throwing three darts each, trying to reduce their starting scores from 501 points to exactly zero points. Dartboards are divided into twenty numbered sections from 1 to 20; each section scores its labeled number. Each section is subdivided into smaller "double point" and smaller still "triple point" areas, scoring the namesake amount of points (for example, a dart striking triple 4 scores 12 points). The center of all dartboards has an outer ring worth 25 points and an inner ring (called the bull's eye) worth 50 points. Dartboards are typically hung at average eye level (5 feet, 8 inches) with the throwing line, behind which players must stand, marked on the floor 7 feet, 9¼ inches from the dartboard wall.

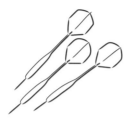

The highest score per throwing turn is 180 points (three darts in triple 20), and it takes a minimum of nine throws to go from 501 to zero points. The tricky bit is that competitors must end exactly on a score of zero, with the final dart landing either on a double or the bull's eye. Otherwise, the player loses their turn and all points earned in the turn.

Given the sport's popularity in pubs, it's no shocker that the sport's top professional players come from Scotland, England, and Wales. Hands-down the world's top player is England's Phil Taylor, who has won a remarkable fifteen world darts championship titles over his career.

SHOOTING

----- BRINGING SHOTGUNS TO THE OLYMPICS -----

SHOOTING WAS ONE OF THE ORIGINAL NINE OLYMPIC SPORTS when the modern games debuted in 1896. Shooting remains a full-medal sport today, with competitions in both air pistol and air rifle (weapons that use gas propellant, as opposed to live ammunition) at distances of 10 meters, 25 meters, and 50 meters. Shooters must display a variety of skills, from shooting in prone position (lying flat) to standing positions. Besides the Olympics the main competition for pistol and rifle marksmanship are the annual World Shooting Championships and World Cup, both hosted by the International Shooting Sports Federation (ISSF; www.issf-sports.org).

The Olympics also offers medals in three shotgun shooting categories: trap, double trap, and skeet. All involve shooting clay targets from a fixed standing position using a shotgun (live pigeons were used at the 1896 Olympics—not great from a publicity perspective). Trap involves hitting a single target released at high speeds away from the shooter. Double trap uses two targets. Either way, shooters are allowed only one shot per target. Skeet uses a series of targets, launched at different heights and speeds, and the shooter must hit as many targets as possible within each series.

Water Sports

CHAPTER TWENTY-FOUR

COMPETITIVE SWIMMING

----- DIFFERENT STROKES FOR DIFFERENT FOLKS -----

★ **BACKSTROKE: BASIC CONCEPT**

The backstroke, one of four swimming styles contested at the
Olympics, made its first appearance at the 1900 Olympics. The
backstroke is unique in that swimmers start in the water (all other
swimming events start with a dive into the pool) and, somewhat
awkwardly, swimmers can't see where they're going! Swimmers in
competition are allowed to turn their heads, but this burns precious
time and energy. Instead, the most skillful swimmers know exactly
how many strokes it takes them to cross the pool and initiate an
under-water turn. Backstroke swimmers have powerful arms, since
the arms generate nearly all the forward movement. The feet are

used more for stabilization and balance, and contribute only a little forward motion.

Backstroke events at the Olympics include 100-meter and 200-meter events for men and women, as well as team medley events with backstroke included as one of the swimming legs.

★ **BREASTSTROKE: BASIC CONCEPT**

The breaststroke looks easy, but it's commonly regarded as the hardest of the four swimming strokes featured at the Olympics. The hallmarks of the breaststroke are the lack of rotation in the torso (breaststroke swimmers keep their torsos as straight as possible for maximum forward movement) and the fact that, even at Olympic levels, swimmers lift their heads above water on each stroke.

The breaststroke derives most of its forward movement from the kick, with the legs whipping back and propelling the body forward. For this reason breaststroke swimmers have seriously powerful leg muscles. Races begin with swimmers diving into the water, and rules allow for 15 meters of underwater swimming before the head must break the surface (in breaststroke races, swimmers instead are allowed a fixed number of underwater strokes). Breaststroke events at the Olympics include 100-meter and 200-meter competitions for men and women, as well as team medley events.

★ **BUTTERFLY: BASIC CONCEPT**

The butterfly stroke is synonymous with the synchronous over-the-head arm rotation that pulls the body forward at great speeds. That, along with a synchronous leg kick, makes the "'fly" one of the fastest and most demanding strokes swum at the Olympics. Partly it's because the butterfly is not easy to become strong enough to master. It can take years of practice to become strong enough master the technique.

The butterfly is a relatively new stroke, invented in Australia at the turn of the twentieth century and modified in the USA in the 1930s for use at swimming competitions. The stroke became a full-medal event starting at the 1956 Olympics and today is one of the four strokes contested at every summer Olympics, in competitions of 100 and 200 meters for both men and women.

★ FREESTYLE: BASIC CONCEPT

Competitive freestyle swimming, as the name suggests, means swimmers can use any swimming style. Despite the theoretical freedom—Olympic freestyle swimmers could do the dog paddle, there's no rule against it!—competitive freestyle swimmers universally use the front-crawl stroke because it's proven to be the fastest.

The front crawl is a simple stroke, and competitions can be dramatic with swimmers milliseconds behind their competitors, eyeing each other as their head turns sideways on each breath. Among the few rules governing freestyle competitions are that swimmers must touch the end of the pool on each lap and at the end of the race, and cannot push off the bottom. Freestyle events start with a dive entry and swimmers are allowed to swim underwater for 15 meters before the head must break the surface. They can also swim 15 meters underwater after each turn.

There are more freestyle events at the Olympics than all other strokes combined: races are contested at distances of 50, 100, 200, 400, 800 (women only), and 1,500 (men only) meters, plus 100-meter and 200-meter freestyle medleys where teams of four swimmers compete for the best overall time.

SYNCHRONIZED SWIMMING

----- DON'T CALL IT WATER BALLET -----

SYNCHRONIZED SWIMMING, AN OLYMPIC MEDAL EVENT since 1984, is one of only three women-only Olympic sports along with rhythmic gymnastics and softball (sadly, softball was dropped from the 2012 Olympics). The sport blends elements of dance and gymnastics in choreographed performances. Teams of two (duet) or eight (team) perform technical routines that require moves in a specific order, as well as freestyle routines that have no requirements and allow swimmers to focus on innovative choreography.

The typical synchronized routine features leg and arm choreography, as well as lifts and throws integrated into creative grouping combinations. At all times swimmers must synchronize with each other and with the music, and swimmers are never allowed to touch bottom.

PLATFORM DIVING

PLATFORM DIVING, AN OLYMPIC EVENT SINCE 1904, is perennially popular among spectators—both live and on television. The sport is a highly telegenic blend of grace and skillful technique with plenty of drama. It's nerve-wracking for spectators and divers alike as divers ascend the 10-meter tower and peer thoughtfully over the platform's edge, mentally preparing themselves for a flying-forward, one-and-a-half-somersault performance.

In platform competitions divers are allowed to jump from heights of 5, 7.5, or 10 meters, though only 10-meter heights are performed at the Olympics. In all cases divers are scored on three elements of their dive: the approach, the flight, and the entry into the water.

★ **BASIC CONCEPT:**

Competitive platform divers perform a predetermined number of dives and are scored by a panel of judges (usually seven judges, with the highest and lowest scores discarded) on a scale of 0 to 10 points. The raw score for every dive is multiplied by a degree of difficulty, a standard calculation based on the number and difficulty of the movements attempted. The diver with the highest overall score wins.

Divers are judged on every aspect of the dive, from the approach to the in-air flight to entry into the water (the rules for the latter require a diver enter the water vertically and create as little splash as possible). Divers can earn a maximum 3 points for approach and takeoff, 3 points for the flight, 3 points for entry, and 1 point at the discretion of the judge.

There are six dive groups in platform competitions: forward (jump forward and rotate forward), back (start with back to water and rotate backward), inward (back to the water and rotate forward), reverse (jump forward and rotate backward), twist (any dive with an axial twisting movement), and armstand (starting from a handstand).

During the flight, divers must assume one of four positions: straight (no bending at knees or hips), pike (straight knees, tight bend at hips), tuck (holding shins, toes pointed, body in a ball), or free (a dive with a twist, incorporating combinations of straight, pike, and tuck positions).

VARIANT » SPRINGBOARD DIVING

Springboard diving was introduced to the Olympics in 1908, just four years after platform diving. At nearly every Olympics since then the diving program has included 1-meter and 3-meter springboard competitions (the numbers refer to height above the water), as well as the 10-meter platform competition.

The real differences between platform and springboard diving are the heights (platform dives start from a much higher position and offer divers a longer flight time) and the approach (springboard dives utilize a flexible board that propels divers into the air). Otherwise, in terms of scoring and dive movements, the two sports are essentially identical.

Synchronized diving is the newest Olympic diving category: it was added as a full-medal event at the 2000 games in Sydney. As the name suggests, synchronized diving features a team of two divers jumping simultaneously. Each set of dives is scored on overall execution as well as on the synchronization of the divers' movements.

SURFING

----- IT'S AN ATTITUDE, BRO -----

SURFING CAN BE A LIFESTYLE, AN ATTITUDE, a way of life—and occasionally it can be a competitive sport, too. A small band of professional surfers trek from competition to competition, earning points and climbing up the rankings of the Association of Surfing Professionals (ASP; www.aspworldtour.com), the sport's governing body.

Surfing is generally divided into shortboard and longboard styles, based on the type of board in use. The former are usually 6 to 7 feet long and give surfers extra control due to the board's tight turning radius. Longboards today are 9 to 12 feet long and are known for their stability.

Professional shortboard surfers compete for the title of ASP World Tour Champion, which has been dominated in recent years by surfers like Kelly Slater on the men's side and Stephanie Gilmore and Layne Beachley on the women's side. There are also annual tournaments to determine the world's best longboarding surfers, and events such as the Vans Hawaiian Triple Crown where men and women compete in three different big-wave locations on the Hawaiian island of Oahu.

WATERSKIING

----- HIT IT! -----

LIKE SURFING, WATERSKIING IS A POPULAR LEISURE ACTIVITY and an occasional competitive sport. Waterskiing's heyday was in the 1970s (the sport took off in the early '70s partly as a result of being included as a demonstration sport at the 1972 Summer Olympics). Nowadays it's a niche sport with small television audiences but a loyal fan base.

Competitive waterskiing covers a range of skills: slalom, race, show, jump, and trick skiing are the most popular. In slalom races, skiers earn points for completing a course with fixed buoys acting as slalom gates. In race skiing, boat-and-skier teams compete for the fastest times around a fixed course. In show skiing, teams of skiers perform gymnastic-style acrobatics including human pyramids and jumps. Jump skiing is similar to its snow-jump cousin; waterski jumpers compete for the longest distances in the air. Trick skiing is not unlike freestyle snowboarding, with skiers judged on the complexity and difficulty of their maneuvers.

WATER POLO

----- RUGBY MEETS ICE HOCKEY, IN A SWIMMING POOL -----

MANY PEOPLE ARE SURPRISED THAT WATER POLO has a long, illustrious history and has been played at every Olympic games since 1900. The sport took shape in the late nineteenth century in England and Scotland and its boosters promoted it as an aquatic version of rugby. No surprise, water polo has always been an aggressive sport. Underwater kicks, hindering an opponent, intentional splashing— it's all part of the game, as long as the referee doesn't call a foul!

Water polo is also a physically demanding sport. Swimmers are constantly on the move, treading water and using leg movements such as the "egg beater" to propel their body out of the water to gain elevation and a clear shot on goal.

★ **BASIC CONCEPT:**

Water polo matches are contested by two teams of seven (six players and one goalie in the water per side). Teams score points by throwing a ball into the opponent's net. The goalie is the only player allowed to touch the ball with both hands; all other players move the ball with one hand or push it forward with the upper body as they swim.

Teams cannot have possession of the ball for more than 30 seconds without attempting a shot on goal. Shots are made by skipping or bouncing the ball so that, ideally, it deflects on the water's surface up into the goal. Lob shots are also common, where a player throws the ball in a high arc that forces the goalie to propel up and back to block the ball out (harder than it sounds when you're constantly treading water).

Water polo games are divided into quarters that last 8 minutes at the Olympics level. The game clock does not stop for possession changes or minor fouls, but it does stop for penalty shots and after a goal is scored. At the end of the game the team with the higher score wins. Ties are broken by playing two 3-minute overtime periods. If the game is still tied a penalty shootout determines the winner (five players from each side shoot penalty shots).

★ **RULES AND TERMINOLOGY:**

Fouls are common in water polo and come in two categories: standard fouls that cause a change in possession but do not stop the game clock, and more serious fouls that result in ejection from the pool. Ejections create six-on-five power plays, where the penalized team temporarily plays at a disadvantage. If a major foul is committed within 5 meters of the goal, the opposing team is awarded a penalty shot. If a player earns three major fouls, they're ejected for the remainder of the game.

25

★ ⋯⋯ 25 ⋯⋯ ★

Wrestling and Weightlifting

CHAPTER TWENTY-FIVE

FREESTYLE WRESTLING

----- THE ULTIMATE TAKEDOWN -----

WRESTLING IS ONE OF THE WORLD'S OLDEST RECORDED SPORTS (references go as far back as the twelfth century BC). The sport takes many forms, including the freestyle version which has been contested at every Olympics since 1904. In freestyle matches, wrestlers from the same weight class (wrestlers are divided into seven weight classes from 110 to 260 pounds) take to the wrestling mat and compete in three 2-minute rounds.

In each round wrestlers earn points for throws resulting in takedowns, in reversals (gaining control over an opponent from a weaker position), and in exposing an opponent's back to the mat without achieving a complete pin. A match ends immediately if one wrestler is able to pin his opponent's shoulders to the mat for 2 seconds (this is called a fall or pin). Otherwise the match is won by the wrestler who wins two out of three rounds.

Women's freestyle wrestling was introduced as a full-medal sport at the 2004 Olympics.

GRECO-ROMAN WRESTLING

----- ALL AIR, ALL THE TIME -----

GRECO-ROMAN WRESTLING MADE ITS DEBUT at the very first modern Olympics in 1896, and it's been a full-medal sport in every Olympic games since 1908. The key difference between freestyle and Greco-Roman is the latter forbids the use of holds below the waist. Competitors use a variety of throws and upper-body grapples to score takedowns, but cannot use their feet or legs to bring their opponent's shoulders to the mat. All the action in Greco-Roman wrestling is in the air. In nearly all other respects, the rules of Greco-Roman mirror those governing freestyle wrestling.

OIL WRESTLING

----- OLIVE OIL, OF COURSE -----

DESPITE RUMORS TO THE CONTRARY, oil wrestling is not the same thing as mud wrestling! The national sport of Turkey is not to be confused with buxom blondes wrestling while slathered in mud. Oil wrestling is a major sport and extremely competitive. In fact, competitions have been held in Turkey most every year since the late 1370s, making it planet Earth's oldest continuously contested sport.

Wrestlers, called *pehlivans*, wear leather waist harnesses called *kisbets* and coat their bodies with olive oil to make themselves harder to grab or grapple. The general idea is for a wrestler to completely control his opponent by pinning him to the ground using the kisbet for leverage. In the old days matches could last days at a time until one wrestler finally dominated a rival; today matches are limited to a single 30-minute round plus an extra 10-minute period in case of ties. Matches are typically held outside on open fields.

SUMO

JAPAN IS THE SPIRITUAL AND PROFESSIONAL HOME OF SUMO (which is tied with baseball as Japan's most popular sport). The sport has existed in its current form since Japan's Edo period in the early seventeenth century. The rules are exceedingly simple. Two wrestlers enter a circular ring (called a *dohyo*) roughly 15 feet in diameter and made of clay. The winner is the first wrestler to push his opponent outside the ring or to force his opponent to touch the ground with any part of the body other than the soles of his feet.

Wrestlers wear only a thick belt, used by an opponent to grasp and leverage an opponent out of the ring. There are seventy official moves used to beat an opponent, including overarm and underarm throws. Wrestlers can also trip or slap with an open hand. Some of the few restrictions include eye gouging, hair pulling, and hitting with a closed fist.

Sumo's simplicity in the ring is paired with a host of complex rituals outside the ring. The Japanese Sumo Association (Nihon Sumo Kyokai; www.sumo.or.jp/eng/) manages nearly every aspect of a professional sumo wrestler's life: what they eat, what they wear, even how they live (in communal training compounds).

The Sumo Association recognizes six divisions based on ability (as opposed to weight) and tightly controls the numbers of wrestlers officially ranked in each category. Across all of Japan fewer than 700 sumo wrestlers are allowed to compete professionally. Six Grand Sumo tournaments (called *honbasho*) are held annually, each lasting fifteen days. On each day of the tournament wrestlers perform the "entering the ring" ceremony (called the *dohyo-iri*) wearing colorful ceremonial aprons. Before each match wrestlers typically throw salt into the air and then clap hands to attract the attention of the gods, extending palms upward to show the deities they are not concealing any weapons! The ceremony ends with a leg lift and ceremonial foot-stomp in the dohyo to drive evil from the ring.

On the amateur side, the International Sumo Federation (ISF; www.amateursumo.com) organizes sumo matches around the world and hosts the annual amateur Sumo World Championships.

BIGGER? YES. BETTER? NOT REALLY.

IN THE 1950S THE AVERAGE SUMO WRESTLER weighed 317 pounds. Nowadays the average weight of a wrestler is more than 405 pounds! Obesity is a serious concern in sumo circles, especially since the average life span of a wrestler is twelve years shorter than that of the average Japanese man.

WEIGHTLIFTING

----- A JERK IN THE NICEST SENSE -----

COMPETITIVE WEIGHTLIFTING IS A POPULAR INTERNATIONAL SPORT and has regularly featured at every summer Olympics since 1920

(women's weightlifting made its Olympics debut in 2000). The sport's governing body, the International Weightlifting Federation (IWF; www.iwf.net), has organized its own annual World Weightlifting Championships since 1891. Nowadays professional weightlifters compete in two major categories: snatch and clean-and-jerk.

★   **SNATCH: BASIC CONCEPT**

The goal is to lift a weighted bar from a platform to mid-chest level, flipping the barbell up and positioning the body underneath the bar, then catching it with locked arms in a squatting position before finally standing up straight with the barbell overhead. All in a single fluid movement. Not easy. The world record weight lifted in a snatch competition is a staggering 470 pounds.

★   **CLEAN AND JERK: BASIC CONCEPT**

The "clean" part is lifting the bar from the floor to just below the chin in a squatting position, and then standing upright in preparation for "the jerk." This refers to a forward lunge of the body as the bar is lifted overhead. Lifters must keep their arms locked and their legs directly beneath their torso in a single line. The current world record for clean-and-jerk lifting is 580 pounds.

★ ★ ★ ★ ★
★ ★ ★ ★ ★

26

>>

Ye Olde Sports

CHAPTER TWENTY-SIX

>>

CHARIOT RACING

----- BREAD AND CIRCUSES -----

A SATIRIST IN THE FIRST CENTURY BC NAMED JUVENAL WROTE that "the people [of Rome] hold themselves in check and anxiously desire only two things, their daily bread and chariot races at the Circus." In

other words, the people of ancient Rome exchanged their freedoms for little more than full bellies and violent, low-brow entertainment of the sort typically staged at Rome's Circus Maximus stadium in the heart of the city.

Betting on races was endemic. And while most charioteers started as slaves, successful ones soon earned enough money to purchase their freedom. Racing chariots were designed to be small and lightweight with almost no protection for the riders, who basically balanced on the chariot's axle as they drove their horse or horses around the track seven full times (the length of a standard race).

GLADIATOR COMBAT

----- I'M SPARTACUS! -----

THE NAME *GLADIATOR* COMES FROM A ROMAN SWORD called the gladius—the hallmark weapon in a fight-to-the-death combat pitting criminals, slaves, and prisoners of war against one another in venues like the Forum and Colosseum in Rome. Upper-class Romans were prohibited from being gladiators, though some certainly ignored the law and entered the arena, along with the occasional woman. No matter what class they came from, all gladiators swore the same oath: "I shall endure to be burned, to be bound, to be beaten, and to be killed by the sword."

Gladiators fought in a variety of styles, some on horseback, some with heavy weapons, some with nets. On the day of battle gladiators entered the arena and fought until one combatant wounded or otherwise established dominance over his competitor. At that point the sponsor of the match (often a wealthy nobleman or local politician) would indicate whether the gladiator was to live or die by waving his thumb (signaling death) or pressing his thumb to his hand (sparing the gladiator's life). A gladiator marked for death was expected to accept the coup de grâce blow with honor (no whining, no flinching).

JOUSTING

----- MARYLAND'S OTHER OFFICIAL SPORT? LACROSSE. -----

THE OFFICIAL SPORT OF MARYLAND (GO AHEAD, LOOK IT UP), jousting is the ancient chivalrous art of charging a competitor on horseback and attempting to knock him off his horse with a lance. The sport's heyday was the twelfth to fourteenth centuries in Europe, when armor-clad knights competed for fame and glory—and to earn pay in the service of local nobility. The typical jousting tournament featured dozens of bouts on the "list," or jousting field.

Believe it or not, jousting has made a comeback in the form of horse-based competitions pitting riders attempting to spear small hoops or rings with a lance. And yes, there is a governing body. Say hello to the National Jousting Association (NJA; www.nationaljousting.com).

NAUMACHIA

----- MOCK SEA BATTLES, REAL VIOLENCE -----

NAUMACHIA MEANS "SEA BATTLE" IN LATIN and refers to the mock sea battles staged in ancient Rome on rivers and in water-filled stadiums (it's thought that the Colosseum in Rome was a frequent setting for naumachia battles). Although staged as sporting entertainments, sea battles were very real to the slaves and prisoners of war who were forced to participate—and often die—recreating naval battles between the Romans, Egyptians, Athenians, Persians, and Tyrians.

Battles often included a dozen or more full-sized sailing boats manned by dozens of oarsmen. No surprise, naumachiae were expensive to stage and reserved for only major celebrations, often tied to the military victories of an emperor (Julius Caesar, for example, staged the first known naumachia in 46 BC with more than five thousand rowers and combatants).

PANKRATION

----- WRESTLING MEETS KICKBOXING MEETS -----
MIXED MARTIAL ARTS

PANKRATION IS AN ANCIENT FORM OF MIXED MARTIAL ARTS, a combination of wrestling and no-holds-barred boxing and kickboxing. Pankration was considered an essential warrior skill and was contested at the ancient Olympics on a regular basis. The sport was brutal and had few rules, other than one competitor dominating another with almost no limits on the types of holds, kicks, or grabs allowed. The only prohibited moves were eye-gouging and biting.

Oddly enough, there's plenty of modern nostalgia for the sport (the modern version emphasizes grappling and limited-contact mixed martial arts). The sport's governing body is the USA Federation of Pankration Athlima (USAFPA; www.teamusapankration.com), which was recently recognized by the International Federation of Associated Wrestling Styles (FILA; www.fila-wrestling.com). Boosters consider this recognition the first step on the road to reinstating pankration at the Olympics.

PITZ

THE MAYA PEOPLE, ALONG WITH OTHER PRE-COLUMBIAN PEOPLES of Mesoamerica, played a ball game variously called ulama or pitz. The rules are unknown, though judging from the shape of the ball court (a long rectangle with tall side walls), it's likely that keeping the ball in play was key. The game was played with a ball similar to a volleyball but made from rubber and much heavier. Another hallmark feature is decapitation! It's unclear if losing one's head was a penalty for losing, or a masochistic reward for winning. Either way, many murals from the era feature pitz players literally losing their heads.

SKITTLES

----- THE ART OF THROWING A CHEESE -----

SKITTLES WAS ONCE UBIQUITOUS IN ENGLAND. Throughout the Middle Ages and into the Elizabethan and Tudor periods, skittles was predominantly an outdoor sport where participants rolled or threw a wooden ball (called a cheese) in an attempt to knock down a set of pins (called skittles).

Sometime in the late seventeenth century the sport moved indoors into public houses and bowling alleys (a precursor to nine- and ten-pin bowling, which evolved from skittles). Along the way both the balls and skittles (pins, usually nine in total and arranged in a square formation) shrunk in size, and bowling alleys were replaced by long wooden tables (similar to shuffleboard tables). Skittles is still played in parts of England, usually over a pint and often for small wagers.

TUG OF HOOP

----- THE MOTHER OF ALL HOOP ROLLING SPORTS -----

THERE IS PLENTY OF EVIDENCE THAT THE ANCIENT EGYPTIANS were sports lovers. The trick is, few rules have survived and many of the sports remain fuzzy in terms of their objective. Case in point is the tug of hoop. Numerous engravings and paintings from four thousand years ago depict two men using hooked staffs to push or control a hoop made of wood or woven reeds. It seems the goal was to snatch the hoop from the competitor without letting the hoop fall over. Or maybe not; it's hard to know. The ancient Egyptians forgot to leave us a rulebook.

TUG OF WAR

----- PULL. HARDER. -----

IT'S QUITE POSSIBLE THAT TUG OF WAR is the oldest competitive sport still played today. The origins of tug of war extend back thousands of years and across dozens of ancient cultures from Egypt to China, India to Japan, Korea to Hawaii. Engravings and ancient carvings from dozens of cultures depict teams of pullers grappling a rope and pulling, in a contest designed to test participants' strength and teamwork skills. Tug of war was not only a team sport; in several countries a man-to-man version existed.

Believe it or not, tug of war was an Olympic sport from 1900 to 1920 and is still featured in competitions worldwide, from the Scottish Highland Games to the Pushkar Camel Fair in India. The Tug of War International Federation (TWIF; www.tugofwar-twif.org) is the sport's governing body and organizes world championships every two years.

ABOUT THE AUTHOR

SCOTT MCNEELY is the author of Chronicle Books' *Ultimate Book of Card Games, Ultimate Book of Jokes,* and *Poker Night.* His writing has appeared in numerous magazines, websites, and travel guidebooks. He lives in Portland, Oregon.